P9-EGL-623

NATURE CRAFTS FOR KIDS

NATURE CRAFTS FOR KIDS

GWEN DIEHN & TERRY KRAUTWURST

A Sterling/Lark Book
Sterling Publishing Co., Inc. New York

Editor: Carol Taylor
Art Director: Marcia Winters
Photography: Evan Bracken
Illustrations: Rick Frizzell
Production: Elaine Thompson, Marcia Winters

Library of Congress Cataloging in Publication Data
Diehn, Gwen, [date]
Nature crafts for kids : 50 fantastic things you can make with Mother Nature's help / by Gwen Diehn and Terry Krautwurst.
p. cm.
"A Sterling/Lark book."
Includes index.
Summary: Provides instructions for using leaves, flowers, twigs, and shells to make fifty craft projects, including kites, kaleidoscopes, and clocks.
ISBN 0-8069-8372-8
1. Nature craft--Juvenile literature. [1. Nature craft. 2. Handicraft.] I. Krautwurst, Terry, [date] . II. Title.
TT160.D39 1992
745.5--dc20 91-36387
CIP
AC

ISBN 0-8069-8372-8

10 9 8

A Sterling/Lark Book

Produced by Altamont Press, Inc.
50 College St., Asheville, NC 28801, USA

Published in 1992 by Sterling Publishing Co., Inc.
387 Park Ave. S., New York, NY 10016

Distributed in Canada by Sterling Publishing,
c/o Canadian Manda Group, P.O. Box 920, Station U, Toronto, Ontario M8Z 5P9
Distributed in the United Kingdom by Cassell PLC, Villiers House, 41/47 Strand, London WC2N 5JE, England
Distributed in Australia by Capricorn Link Ltd., P.O. Box 665, Lane Cove, NSW 2066

Printed in Hong Kong

ACKNOWLEDGEMENTS

We'd like to thank the people who contributed additional photography, projects, and sidebars, or who let us use their backyards for location photography. We'd especially like to thank the kids who participated in the book.

ADDITIONAL PHOTOGRAPHY

BRANSON REYNOLDS (Spring, pages 10-11; Rain, page 16; Leaf Canopy, page 61; Autumn, pages 84-85; Mountain with Evergreens, page 90; Winter, pages 114-115). Photographs © Branson Reynolds.
DAN PEHA (Star Trails, page 132). Photograph © Dan Peha
Aramco World magazine (Setting Sun, page 55; Ocean, page 75)
MINISTERE DU TOURISME, Gouvernement du Quebec (Snow Sculptures, pages 118-119)
CORNELL LABORATORY OF ORNITHOLOGY (Bird Eggs, page 29)
VERMONT TRAVEL DIVISION (Fall Foliage, pages 87 and 89)
KANSAS STATE HISTORICAL SOCIETY (Wind Power, pages 22 and 23)
JERICHO HISTORICAL SOCIETY (Snowflake Bentley, pages 120 and 121)

ADDITIONAL PROJECTS

NORA BLOSE (Bath Bags, Pet Collars, Herb Dolls)
CHUCK CONNER (Bug Box)
JAN DAVIS (Onion-Dyed Eggs)
JANET FRYE (Twig-and-Cone Wreath)
CLYDE HOLLIFIELD (Nocture, Pocket Sundial, Pan Pipes)
JUDY HORN (Corn Husk Flowers)
BOB MILLER (Whimmy Diddle)
CLAUDIA OSBY (Wind Vanes)
DIANE WEAVER (Bandanna, Leaf Prints, Gift Tags/Bookmarks/Notecards, Leaf Collection Box)
LAUREL WINTERS (Evergreen Garland, Pomander)

ADDITIONAL SIDEBARS

DAWN CUSICK (Herbs, Drying Flowers)
CLYDE HOLLIFIELD (Finding Casseopeia)

LOCATION PHOTOGRAPHY

FRED AND NORA BLOSE, GRANVILLE AND LOUISE JUSTICE, JEFF AND ALI TAIT, The Cradle of Forestry in the Pisgah National Forest

THE KIDS

ANNA, MARY, AND SARA BRACKEN
Birdbath, Pinch Pots. Anna: Corn Husk Flowers, Garland, Eggs with Pressed Leaves

NANCY CLEMMONS
Notecard, Bandanna, Sand Painting, Leaf Prints, Fish Kites

TEVYA HARLEY
Pinch Pots, Birdbath

JOSH HOWARD
Apple Puppets, Paw Prints, Pocket Sundial, Track Casting

GREGG HUNSUCKER
Pan Pipes, Twig/Cone Wreath, Fish Print, Sunprint, Turnip Lanterns, Fish Kites

MATTHEW, JEREMY, AND EMILY LONDON
Whimmy Diddle (with grandfather Bob Miller). Jeremy: Bark Rubbing

BEN MACKEL
Homemade Paper, Onion-Dyed Eggs, Sand Candles, Wormery

TOYA POPE
Finding Clay, Pinch Pots, Birdbath

MEGAN, PATRICK, AND SIMON TAIT
Birdbath, Finding Clay, Pinch Pots, Sawdust Kiln. Megan: Pooter

KELSEY WEIR
Bug Box, Kaleidoscope, Fish Kites

LAUREL WINTERS
Candied Violets, Soap, Wildflower Candles, Leaf Stained Glass, Fish Kites

This logo denotes projects which can be made with readily available materials or materials commonly found in most homes.

Please note that there is a *Metric Conversion Chart* on page 144 if you need it to understand the measurements used in this book.

Welcome to Nature Crafts for Kids

When you look at a pine cone, what do you see? You might notice its shape and size and color, and that's about all. But when you gather a bunch of pine cones together from the outdoors and make something with them—a wreath, for example—you learn a lot more: how sticky pine cones can be, how prickly some kinds are, how they're put together, how they smell and feel and where you can find the best ones. You become a pine cone wizard. (And you get a nice wreath, too!)

That's the basic idea behind this book. It's for people who like to learn by *doing* as well as by reading and looking. It's for anyone who likes to make things, and for anyone who's interested in the outdoors.

There are dozens of terrific craft projects in these pages. Some of the projects are simple. Others are more challenging and will take a little more time. But each one shows you how to make something that's useful or attractive or just plain interesting. And at the same time, each one helps you see and feel and understand the natural world around you a little better.

So, although we think you'll enjoy reading this book, we mostly hope you'll *use* it. There are a lot of fascinating and rewarding things to make and do here. And in the making and doing, you're going to discover some exciting things about nature, and about how everything in it (including you!) is important and special.

Come on, let's get going!

A Few Tips About the Crafts Projects

■ Read the instructions all the way through at least once before you begin. It really helps to know how to get where you're going before you start!

■ Gather *all* the materials you need, then begin. There's nothing worse than discovering halfway through a project that you can't finish it because you don't have something you really need. Aaargh!

■ We hope that the project instructions are perfectly clear. But if there's something that doesn't make sense to you, do a trial run. Pretend to actually do the project with, say, a piece of scrap paper or a small twig. If the words don't make sense, acting it out usually makes things clear.

■ If you don't have something (a material or tool, for example) that a project calls for, try to think of something that would work just as well. This is important. Adults who do crafts improvise all the time. When they don't have one thing, they look around and think: what else would do the same job?

■ Some of the projects may call for tools or hardware (nails, screws, and so on) that you've never used or even heard of before. Don't let that stop you! Tools aren't mysterious things used only by adults and unavailable to you. Stores carry them and sell them to people who aren't one bit smarter than you are. People who work there will know what a #6 1-1/4 inch wood screw is, or what an awl is, and will find it for you. After you go look at one, you'll know, too. With the right tool, a job that looks hard (maybe even impossible!) becomes easy to do.

■ Don't limit yourself to just the projects in this book. Nature is full of fascinating shapes and patterns and textures that are fun to work with. Flowers, leaves, stones, sand, twigs, shells—crafts materials are everywhere in the outdoors, just waiting for you and your imagination!

■ **Please note: Pay attention to the safety instructions that appear once in a while. We haven't said "Be careful!" every time we tell you to pick up a pair of scissors. So when we *do* point out that you can get hurt unless you follow the instructions carefully, we're serious. Also, sometimes we suggest that you get an adult to help you with a certain step. We say that only when we think it's important.**

SPRING

Cement Birdbath

What You'll Need

- A shovel
- A large plastic garbage can with a lid*
- Plastic wrap
- A 60-pound bag of sand mix concrete
- Water
- A trowel
- A 12-inch x 12-inch piece of chicken wire or hardware cloth
- Metal shears** or wire cutters
- A large plastic or metal tub (or a wheelbarrow) for mixing concrete
- Broken pieces of crockery or china, or seashells, pretty flat rocks,or beach glass for decoration

*Look for a garbage can lid that has a smooth inside with no plastic tabs or deep indentations.
**Metal shears are designed to cut metal. Any good hardware store will have them.

a

c

b

d

What to Do

1. Dig a shallow hole in the ground the size of the garbage can lid, for the lid to rest in. Be sure the hole is level.

2. Line the inside of the can lid with plastic wrap, and place the lid in the shallow hole.

3. Pour the concrete mix into the tub or wheelbarrow. Add a little bit of water at a time, mixing with your trowel as you add.

You can tell when the mix is right: make a hill in the concrete with your trowel, and slice the hill down the middle with your trowel. If the sides of the slice cave in, the mix is too wet. Add more concrete.

If the slice crumbles, the mix is too dry. Add more water.

If the slice stays put, the mix is just right.

4. Shovel an inch-deep layer of concrete into the lid and smooth it with the trowel.

5. Cut the chicken wire or hardware cloth to fit over the concrete, and an inch inside the edge of the concrete, and lay it flat on top of the layer of concrete.

g

6. Shovel in another inch-deep layer of concrete on top of the hardware cloth.

7. Set the garbage can in the center of the concrete. Put 4 inches of water in the can to hold it in place.

8. With the trowel, fill in concrete around the sides of the can, to form the rim of the birdbath. Smooth the edges.

If you want, you can place shells or pieces of broken pottery around the edge, for decoration.

9. Let the concrete set up for around an hour until it's hard enough to hold its shape. Then gently twist the garbage can to remove it. At this point you can press pottery shards or shells into the bottom of the birdbath to decorate it. Be sure to press the pieces in far enough so that the surface is level and there are no sharp edges that could cut a bird's feet.

10. Keep the concrete damp for three days while it sets up. Here's how to do that: Poke sticks into the ground around the birdbath, and drape a piece of plastic (such as an old shower curtain) over the whole project. The plastic will help keep the sun from drying out the concrete. Spray the concrete with water once a day.

11. After three days, when the concrete is hard, remove the birdbath from the mold. To do this, carefully peel the edge of the garbage can lid back in a few places. Flex the plastic to loosen the birdbath, then turn it over and lift the lid off. Peel away the plastic wrap.

12. Place the birdbath on an old tree stump or balance it on three flat rocks. You might also place it flat on the ground in your garden, or drive three pipes into the ground and rest the birdbath on the pipes. Fill it with water, and watch the birds enjoy it. And if you have a cat, you might want to put a bell on its collar, so it doesn't sneak up on the birds.

h

i

j

RAIN FACTS

■ It takes about nine days for water to evaporate from the oceans or the surface of the earth, condense as part of a cloud, and fall to earth again as rain or snow.

■ There are about one million cloud droplets in one raindrop.

■ The biggest raindrops measure about 1/4 of an inch across.

■ One inch of rain over one square mile weighs about 72,000 tons.

■ Scientists estimate that 40 million gallons of water in the form of rain, snow, or freezing rain fall on the earth every second.

■ The wettest place in the world is Mount Waialeale, on the island of Kauai, Hawaii. It rains there an average of 335 days a year, and sometimes as often as 350 days. The total amount of rain each year averages 460 inches, or more than 38 feet!

■ The driest places in the world are in Chile, South America. In Desierto de Atacama, virtually no rain fell for more than 400 years. In 1972, though, a downpour swept through and caused heavy flooding and mud slides. The village of Arica, in northern Chile, is almost always rainless. It gets an average of 3/100 of an inch of rain a year.

■ The greatest rainfall in one day (24 hours): 73 inches (that's over six feet!), in Cilaos, La Reunion, an island in the Indian Ocean.

■ The greatest rainfall in one year: 1,042 inches, at Cherrapunji, Meghalaya, India, between August 1, 1860 and July 31, 1861. Cherrapunji also holds the record for most rain in one month: 366 inches, in July, 1861. Most years, though, the village gets "only" about 425 inches of rain all together.

RAIN AND CLOUDS

Everybody knows that rain comes from clouds. But where do clouds come from? And why does rain fall from them?

Clouds are actually made up of trillions of tiny drops of water. Water is always in the air, in the form of an invisible gas we call water vapor. The warmer the air, the more water it can hold as vapor. The colder the air, the less water it can hold.

Whenever there's more water in the air than the temperature will allow it to hold, the water vapor condenses: It changes from gas to very small droplets of water. Together, those droplets make a cloud. That's why you can see your breath in the winter when you breathe out, but not during the summer. On a cold day, the air can't hold all the water in your breath, so the vapor condenses and makes a little cloud.

The same thing is going on when clouds form in the sky. Have you noticed that there are usually more clouds over mountains and hills? That's because when air passes over mountains, it's swept upward. The higher it gets, the colder it gets. The air can't hold as much water. So the water condenses and creates clouds.

The ocean is another place where you see a lot of clouds. That's because the air is so full of water from the sea that it condenses even when the air is quite warm.

Rain happens when water droplets in a cloud become heavy enough to fall. Sometimes enough cloud droplets bump into each other and stick together to make larger, heavier droplets that fall. That's usually the cause of short, hard showers during the summer or in tropical places. Long periods of rain or drizzle happen when the water vapor in very high, cold clouds sticks to ice particles and freezes, making heavier ice crystals and snowflakes. When the flakes drop down through warmer air, they melt and fall as rain. (Of course, in cold weather they don't melt, and drift to the ground as snow!)

BAROMETER

What You'll Need

- ■ A glass jar with a wide mouth (2-1/2 to 3 inches across)
- ■ Acrylic paints and a brush
- ■ A 14-inch balloon*
- ■ Scissors
- ■ A piece of string about 12 inches long
- ■ A plastic drinking straw
- ■ Tape
- ■ An 8-inch x 12-inch piece of posterboard
- ■ Markers

*Check the bag the balloon comes in to find out its size. Most balloons are 9 inches; be sure this is a 14-inch one.

What to Do

1. With the brush and acrylic paint, paint designs on the jar. Let it dry.
2. Cut the skinny end off the balloon.
3. Stretch the balloon over the mouth of the jar. Pull it tight so that no bumps remain and the surface is as near perfectly flat as possible.
4. Wrap the string around the mouth of the jar, over the balloon, and tie the string, to help hold the balloon in place.
5. Cut both ends of the straw at angles.
6. Tape one end of the straw flat against the center of the balloon with a small piece of tape.
7. Fold the posterboard in thirds, and tape it into a long triangular column.
8. Stand the posterboard column next to, but not touching, the tip of the straw. Make a small mark on the column where the tip of the straw is pointing.
9. After a few hours, check the barometer. If the tip of the straw is pointing higher or lower on the column, make a mark where it is pointing. Check the weather, and make a symbol to indicate it. You might draw a small sun or a cloud, raindrops or snowflakes. Or you might use colored dots or write out the weather in words.
10. Continue to check the barometer every few hours for a couple of days (or longer if the weather stays the same). Each time the tip points to a new place, make a mark and note the weather. Soon you will begin to notice a pattern, and you won't need to make any new marks.

You'll notice that when the tip of the straw is on its way up, a certain kind of weather follows. When the tip is going down, a different kind of weather follows. Use your barometer to predict the weather.

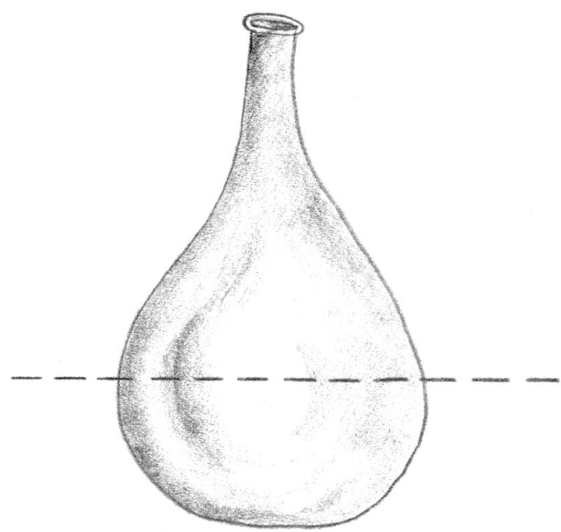

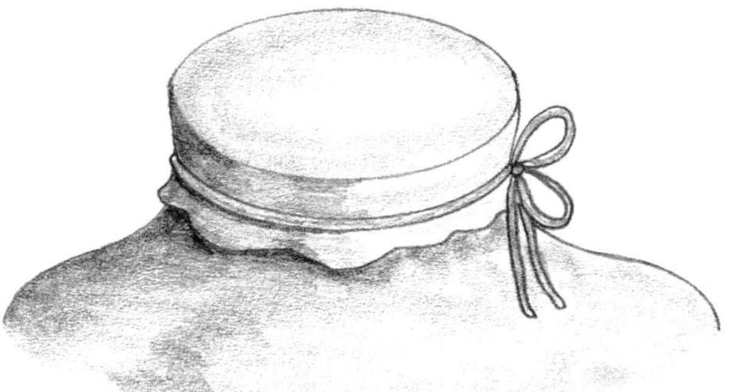

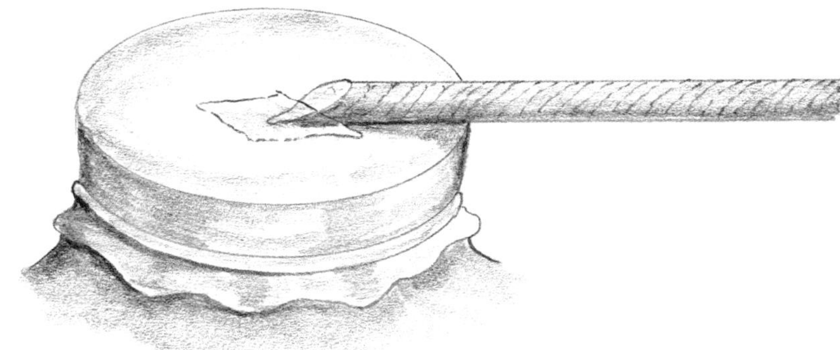

HOW IT WORKS

Air is made up of tiny particles called molecules. There is air inside the jar, held in by the balloon. No air can escape, and no extra air molecules can get inside. The molecules inside the jar press against the balloon, as well as against the sides and bottom of the jar.

There is also air outside the jar, and the outside molecules also press on the balloon. When the pressure inside the jar is less than the pressure outside the jar, then the air outside the jar presses hard enough on the balloon that it pushes in on it. When the balloon is pressed down, the straw tilts upward.

When the pressure inside the jar is greater than the pressure outside the jar, the inside air pushes against the stretchy balloon and causes it to bulge outward. When the balloon bulges outward, the straw tilts down.

Different weather conditions appear with changes in air pressure. Watch your barometer to see which kinds of weather go with high pressure (the straw tip points up) and which kinds of weather go with low pressure (the tip points down).

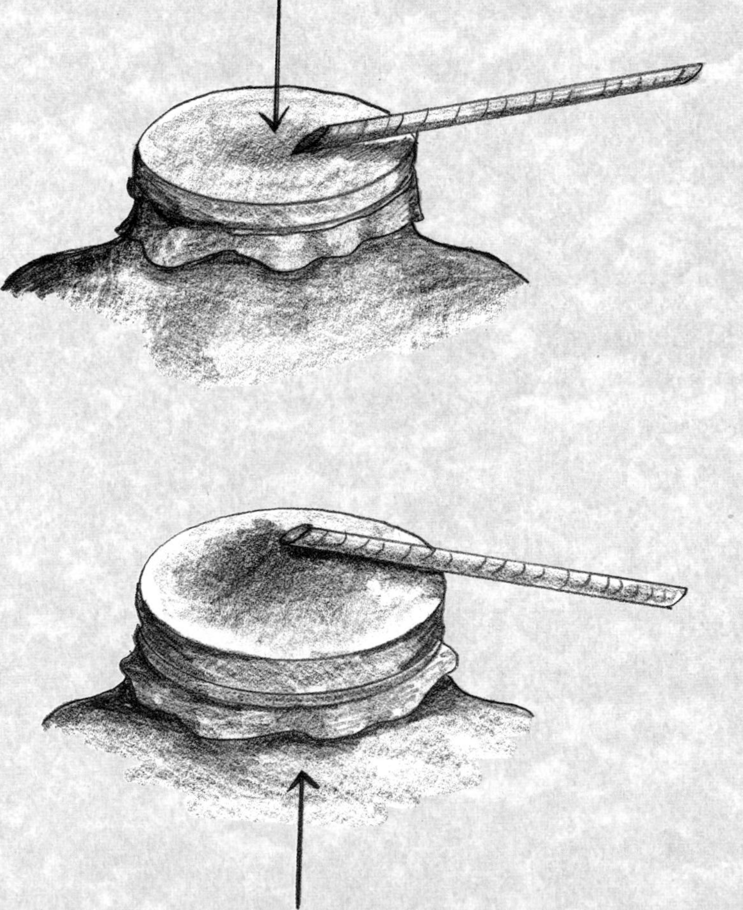

WIND VANE

If you've got a cat, you could use the cat pattern and paint the wind vane to look like your own pet. (All cats are shaped pretty much alike.) If you've got a dog, though, it may not be shaped much like the pattern. You could either use the pattern given, or draw a new one shaped more like your own dog. Then paint it the colors of your pet.

What You'll Need

- Tracing paper
- Pastel crayon or a graphite pencil*
- A piece of 1/4"-thick plywood big enough for the animal. (Our dog measures about 17" x 7", our cat about 12" long and 11" high.)
- A 3/4" x 4" x 26" board
- A saw
- Sandpaper
- Wood sealer
- Acrylic paints
- Paint brushes
- Screw eye and bell (optional)
- A 1-1/4" long piece of brass tubing and a 2" piece of brass rod to fit inside
- A hacksaw
- Carpenter's glue

*These are sold in art supply stores

What to Do

1. Enlarge the pattern to the size you want on a photocopy machine that enlarges. Or draw your own.
2. Trace the pattern onto tracing paper, using a pastel crayon or a graphite pencil—something that rubs off.
3. Lay the pattern on the plywood, crayoned side down, and rub the back of the paper gently, to transfer the pattern to the plywood.
4. Cut out the plywood animal.
5. Sand the cutout, and coat it with wood sealer. (Most kinds are applied with a paint brush.)
6. Paint the animal the colors of your choice. Don't forget to add nose, mouth, whiskers, eyes, and a collar in a contrasting color.
7. If you like, attach a small bell to a tiny screw eye, and screw it into the bottom of the collar.
8. Cut out the three base pieces—the center and both ends of the arrow—from the 3/4" x 4" board.
9. Get an adult to make a 1/4" wide groove 1/2" deep down one 3/4" edge of the board. The bottom of the animal will fit into this slot. This step will take either a power saw or a router.
10. Glue the front and back pieces of the arrow to the base, using carpenter's glue. Slide the animal into its slot, and glue it in place. Let dry.
11. Paint the base the same color as the collar.
12. Drill a hole 1-1/4" deep in the bottom of the weathervane, about 4" back from the wide point of the arrowhead.
13. With a hacksaw, cut a piece of brass tubing 1-1/4" long, and insert it into the hole.
14. Cut a piece of brass rod 2" long. Hammer it 1" into whatever you want the wind vane to sit on—a fence-post, for example. Lower the wind vane onto the brass rod, and allow the wind to do its work.

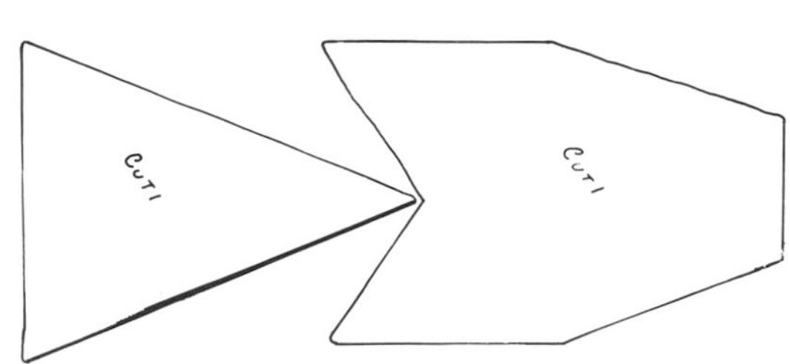

WIND NAMES AROUND THE WORLD

There are lots of different kinds of winds...icy, freeze-your-nose-off winds... sudden gusts that can knock you flat...moist, tropical currents...blasts of hot, sandy, desert air... cool, gentle breezes. People all over the world have given names to the winds. Here are some examples.

HABOOB
In Sudan (a country in Africa) any wind strong enough to create a sand storm.

BRICKFIELDER
Hot, dusty northeast wind that blows during the summer in southeastern Australia.

CHINOOK
Warm, dry, west wind that rushes down the eastern slopes of the Rocky Mountains in the western U.S. and Canada. Chinooks can cause temperatures to rise 20 to 40 degrees in just 15 minutes.

DOLDRUMS
Calm, almost still air near the Equator where northerly and southerly Trade Winds meet. (When people are feeling listless and blue, we sometimes say they're "in the doldrums.")

MISTRAL
Cold, dry, northerly wind that blows off the Mediterranean coasts of Spain and France. Over the centuries, many ships have been lost to mistrals.

WIND POWER

For centuries, the winds moved ships and people and cargo from place to place. Christopher Columbus would never have discovered the New World without wind. Exploring the high seas would have been left to Columbus's great-great-grandchildren, more than 200 years later—after the invention of the steam engine.

But the wind has served more than sailors and explorers. It has been used to grind grain since the 7th century. In fact, we still call almost any machine that's powered by the wind—no matter what job it does—a windmill.

In 15th-century Holland, windmills ran factories that sawed timber, processed wool, and ground spices. Farmers in the United States and Australia have used the wind to pump water to cattle and crops since the mid 1800s. By the early 1900s, there were more than 6 million water-pumping windmills in the U.S.—and there are still thousands operating today.

In the 1920s and 1930s, before electric wires were stretched to almost every community, many farm families in the West and Midwest used small wind generators—windmills that make electricity—to power lights and appliances.

Today, wind power is starting to become popular again. In California, "wind farmers" set up hundreds of wind generators in breezy mountain passes and sell the electricity to the companies that families and businesses get their electricity from. There are now more than 15,000 wind turbines in California, producing enough power to meet the needs of about a million people. California produces 80% of all the world's wind-generated electricity. Denmark produces much of the rest, but Australia, Germany, Spain, the Netherlands, the British Isles, and India also generate large amounts of electricity from the wind.

WHAT MAKES THE WINDS BLOW?

What happens when you blow up a balloon and take your finger off the end? The air whooshes out. That's because when you blew it up you forced air into the balloon under pressure. When you removed your finger, the air did what air does all over the world: move from an area of high pressure (inside the balloon) to an area of lower pressure (the area outside the balloon), in order to even things out.

Now think bigger. Imagine you're ship-wrecked on a tropical

WIND

Without wind, our world would be a completely different place.

Wind spreads the sun's heat around. If breezes didn't blow and air didn't move, more than half of the land on our planet would be too hot for plants to grow. And most of the rest of the earth's surface would be too cold. Nearly two-thirds of the United States would be under ice!

Wind also brings water to plants, animals, and people. Most of the world's moisture comes from the oceans, where it evaporates into the air. The wind blows that moisture in the form of clouds and water vapor to land, where it falls as rain, dew, snow, or ice.

Honeybees usually get the credit for helping plants reproduce by spreading pollen from flower to flower and tree to tree, but wind is really the world's most important pollinator. All evergreens (such as pines, hemlocks, and spruces), and many other trees, including all oaks and birches, rely on the wind to do the job. So do grasses and grains. Without wind, farmers couldn't grow wheat for flour and bread.

And just think of all the seeds you've seen blowing in the wind! Puffy dandelion "parachutes," maple-seed "helicopters," and hundreds of other kinds of seeds are scattered near and far by the wind. In fact, the wind sows more seeds than any other force in nature.

In other words, we have the wind to thank for earth's gentle climate, and for making life possible for most animals and plants—including the ones we humans use for food (such as milk and meat), for clothing (wool and cotton), and for shelter (lumber from trees).

---

island. As you lie on the beach in the morning, the sun rises higher and higher in the sky. The sand gets hotter and hotter. You get hotter and hotter. The air over the island gets hotter and hotter. And because that hot air weighs less than cold air, it rises—just like the air in a hot-air balloon. Result: There's less air pushing down on the surface of your island.

Meanwhile, out over the ocean, the air is cooler—heavier. It's pushing down more. In other words, the pressure is higher.

So just as you're starting to think, "Whew, it's really hot here," a cool breeze blows steadily in from the ocean—air rushing from a high-pressure area to a low-pressure area, just as it does when you loosen your grip on a balloon. That's why there's almost always a breeze blowing in from the sea when you go to the beach. Ahhh, paradise.

All over the world, wherever there's enough difference in temperature to create a difference in air pressure between two places, the wind blows from high to low trying to keep things equal. And the bigger the difference in pressure, the harder the wind.

Fish Kites

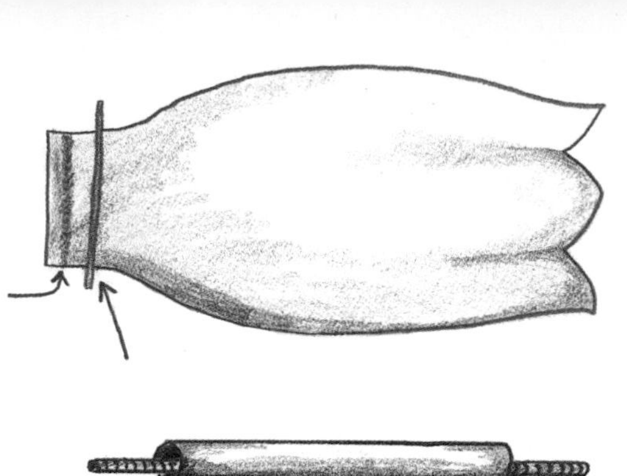

What You'll Need

- ■ Bright colored tissue paper in large sheets*
- ■ Scissors
- ■ A glue stick
- ■ Long pipe cleaners (10 to 12 inches long)
- ■ Sequins, glitter, smaller pieces of colored tissue paper, stick-on dots

*This is available at craft stores and artists' supply stores.

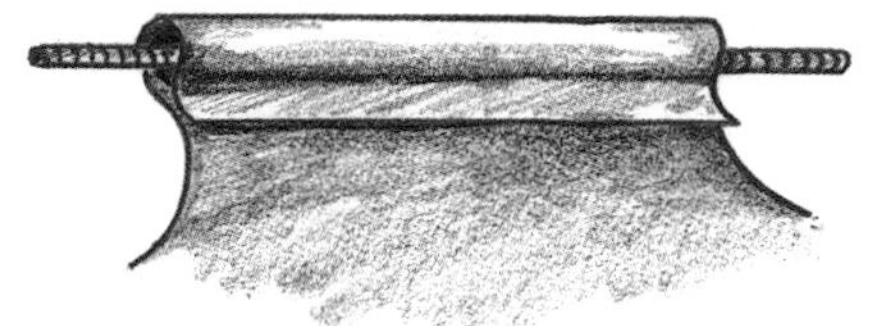

What to Do

1. Fold a piece of tissue paper in half lengthwise. Do *not* crease it.
2. Cut through both layers at one time in the shape shown in the illustration.
3. Unfold the paper.
4. Put a line of glue along the short, straight edge of the paper.
5. Lay a pipe cleaner next to the line of glue (on the side toward the body), then fold the glued paper over the pipe cleaner and press it down.
6. Turn the paper over.
7. Decorate the fish by gluing on some glitter, sequins, or bits of paper, or with stick-on dots sold with office supplies, or with anything you like. Remember that the fish will be folded down the middle, so you'll have to decorate both sides.
8. Holding the kite by the pipe cleaner end, carefully bend the pipe cleaner into a circle, and twist the ends together.
9. Run a line of glue all along one long edge of the fish. Press the other edge of the paper over the glue. Leave the tail end open.
10. Tie kite string to the mouth of the kite to form a bridle.
11. You can tie the bridle to a two-foot-long string and tie the other end of the string to a long pole. Or you can simply use string and run with your fish kite to make it fly.

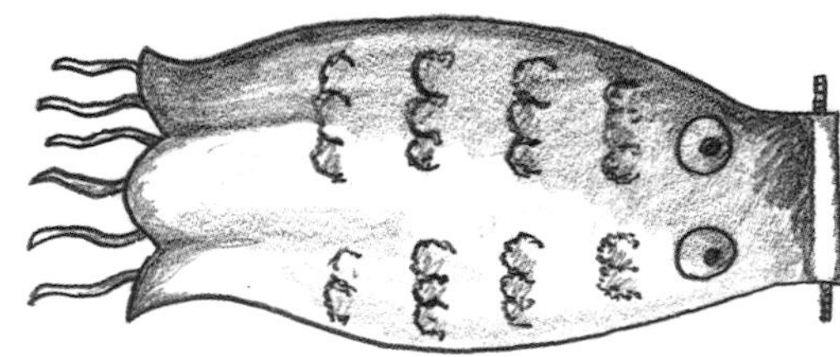

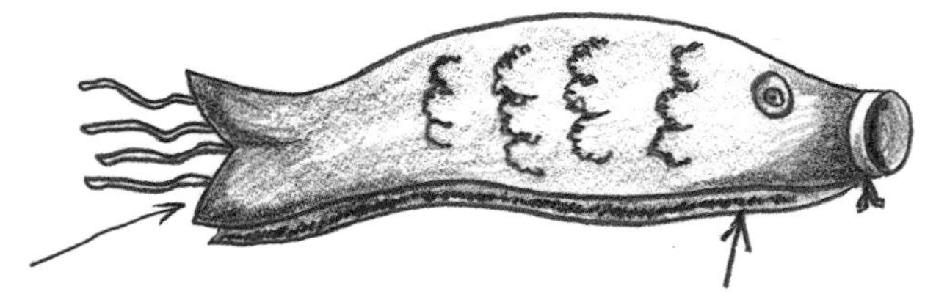

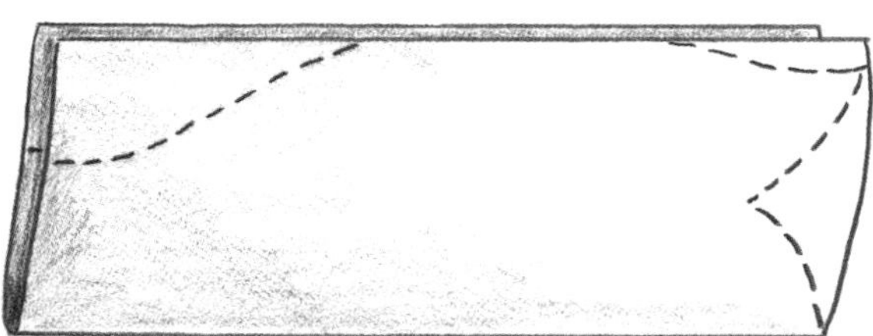

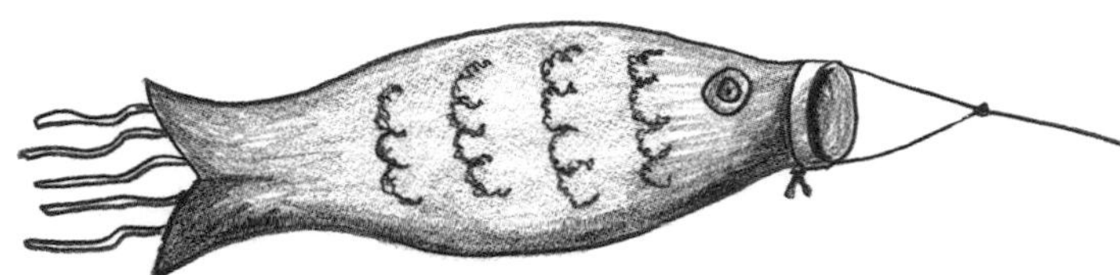

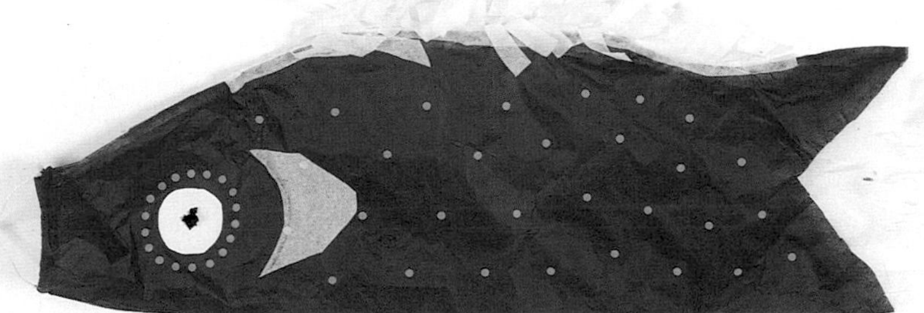

TEXAS NORTHER

Fast-moving, very cold arctic air that sweeps across the Great Plains from Canada into Texas. Texas Northers have been clocked at 70 miles an hour. Temperatures can fall as much as 50 degrees in three hours.

SIROCCO

("SI-ROCK-O")

Stifling hot wind that blows from the Sahara Desert across the north coast of Africa and the Mediterranean Sea to southern Europe, where it is known for making people depressed and irritable. When Italian lawyers defend their clients for doing crazy things, they sometimes "plead the sirocco."

WILLIWAW

In coastal and central Alaska, any brisk wind blowing down off the mountains.

PAMPERA

Extremely cold southerly wind that whips across the prairies (pampas) in Argentina and Uruguay.

SOUTHERLY BUSTER

In Australia, a sudden change from a moderate, relatively warm north wind to a brisk, very cold south wind.

PURGA

In Russia, a fierce northeasterly winter wind that whips snow from the ground into a driving blizzard.

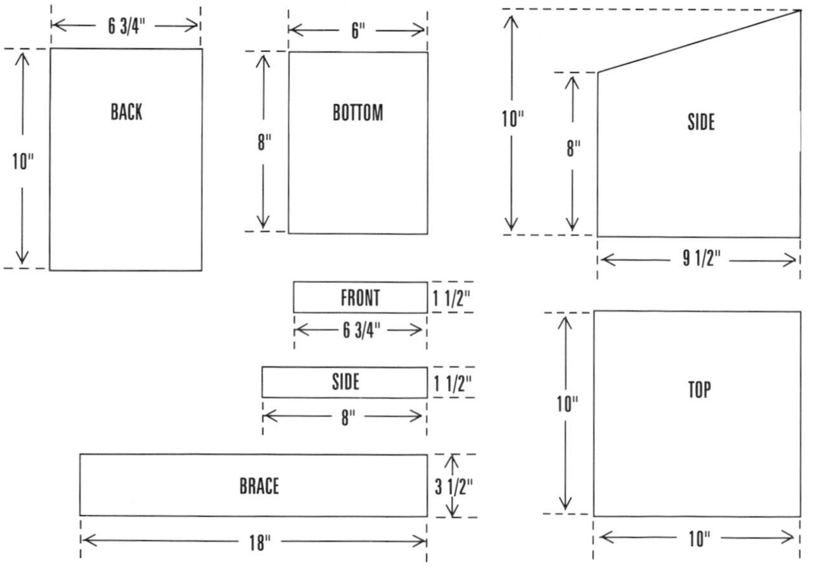

Nesting Shelf

You can attract robins, phoebes, and barn swallows to your home with nesting shelves like this one. It provides a good, safe place for such birds to raise a family. And it's open on two sides, so you get to watch the birds build their nest, lay their eggs, and take care of their young.

What You'll Need

- One 4-foot-long 1 X 12 pine or fir board
- 14 to 18 1-1/2" 4-penny finishing nails
- A saw
- Sandpaper
- A drill
- A hammer
- House paint or wood stain

What to Do

1. Saw the parts of the nesting shelf (top, back, bottom, front, sides, and brace) to the sizes shown in the drawing. Measure carefully before you cut!
2. Drill holes around the bottom, or floor, of the nesting shelf so that rain and moisture can drain away.
3. Sand all the pieces. Make sure the edges are smooth.
4. Paint or stain all the parts using neutral-color house paint or wood stain. Be sure to cover both sides and all four edges of each piece.
5. Nail the front and right side pieces to the bottom. Drill 1/16" holes first to avoid splitting the wood.
6. Now (drilling first each time) attach the left side . . . the back . . . the brace . . . and the top.
7. Hang the nesting shelf six to 10 feet up from the ground on a wall or a tree trunk that faces north or northeast, and wait for a family to move in!

Eggs with Pressed Flowers and Leaves

What You'll Need

- Hard-boiled eggs
- Small pressed flowers or leaves
- Rubber cement

What to Do

1. Make sure the eggs are room temperature—neither hot nor cold. Wipe them with a tissue or soft cloth, to remove dust or smudges.
2. Paint a nice even layer of rubber cement where you want the leaf or flower to be.
3. Lay the leaf or flower on the wet rubber cement, and gently pat it down until it is glued flat to the egg.
4. Glue down all the other leaves and flowers that you want on the egg.
5. After the rubber cement has dried, carefully rub away any extra.

A small ball of rubber cement is good for rubbing other cement away. To make a ball, paint a thick stroke or two of rubber cement on a piece of scrap paper. After it dries, rub it into a ball. Add more cement if it's too small to hold. When you get a ball you can grip between two fingers, use it to clean up your egg.

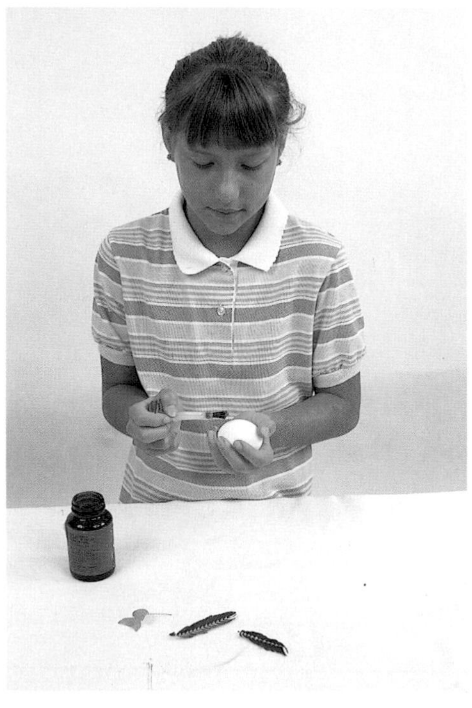

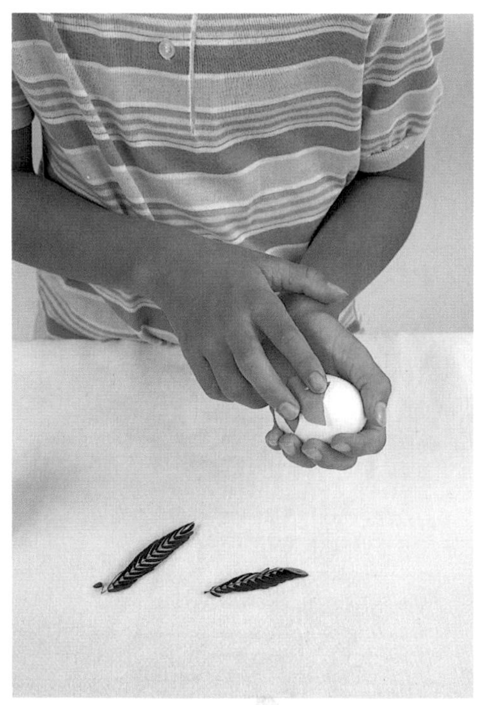

EGG SHAPES AND COLORS

Between the time that it's laid and the time a baby bird hatches out of it, an egg is an accident waiting to happen. But its own special shape and color help to protect it.

Seabirds that build their nests high up on ledges lay eggs that are round on one end and pointed on the other. If a mother bird accidentally bumps into an egg and it starts to roll, it just goes around in a circle instead of falling off the cliff. Owls, on the other hand, live in hollowed-out trees, where there's practically no danger of an egg tumbling out of the nest. Owl eggs are almost perfectly round.

Owl eggs are also white—and so are the eggs of most other birds that nest in holes or dark, covered places. That's because, if the eggs were colored, they'd be hard for the mother to see. She might step on them and break them. Birds that nest in the open, on or near the ground, lay eggs that are camouflaged. They're colored, spotted, or dotted so that they blend in with their surroundings and are hard for egg-eating animals (and other birds) to see.

Eggs of a brown-headed cowbird...

a blue jay...

a robin...

and a whippoorwill.

EGG RECORDS

WORLD'S BIGGEST: ostrich eggs, about 5 inches across and 3-1/2 pounds. (It takes 40 minutes to soft-boil one.)

WORLD'S SMALLEST: vervain hummingbird eggs, about 1/3 inch long and1/100 of an ounce.

MOST LAID IN ONE YEAR: 371, by a hard-working chicken.

Eggs Dyed With Onion Skins

What You'll Need

- Onion skins from yellow or red onions*
- A pan
- White eggs
- Leaves or flowers
- Old pantyhose or knee-highs
- Twist ties

*Your local grocery store will probably let you have the loose skins from the onion bin. You'll need enough to fill a large pan.

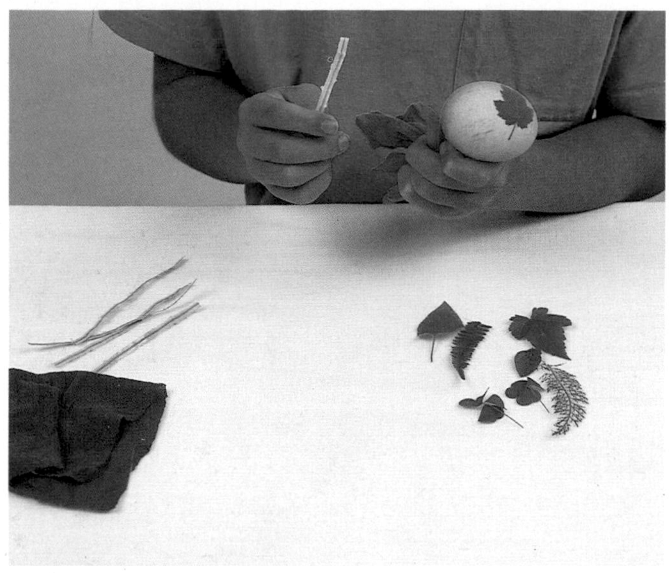

What to Do

1. Put the onion skins in a pan, and add about 3 inches of water (enough to cover the eggs when you add them the next day). Bring the water to a boil, reduce the heat, and simmer the onion skins for about 5 minutes. Remove from the heat and let the pan sit overnight.
2. Cut a piccc of old pantyhose about 6 inches square.
3. Now attach a leaf or flower to an egg. To do that, dip the leaf in water and lay it on the egg. (The water helps hold it in position.) Wrap the square of hosiery over the leaf and around the egg, twisting the hose in back and tying it with a twist tie.
4. Put the wrapped eggs in the pan of dye. Dye only one layer of eggs at a time, and use the wet onion skins to keep the eggs apart.
5. Put the pan of eggs and dye on the stove and bring almost to a boil. Quickly reduce the heat (don't let them bang around, or they might break), and simmer about 30 minutes. Remove them from the heat, let them cool, and unwrap the eggs. Dry them off and coat them with a thin layer of vegetable oil, to make them shiny.
6. You can use the dye over and over again. When you're through with it, you can dump it in the garden, to help mulch the plants.

Finding and Cleaning Clay

What You'll Need

- A trowel
- 2 buckets
- A sieve. If you can't buy one of these, you can make one by nailing together 4 pieces of 1-inch by 2-inch lumber into a square, and then using a staple gun to attach a piece of hardware cloth to the bottom.
- A piece of window screening as big as the sieve or slightly larger
- An old T-shirt
- A piece of plywood at least 3 feet by 3 feet

What to Do

1. The best place to find clay is in the banks of a creek. Walk in the creek and watch for places, low on the bank, where the soil looks slick or slippery. Often clay is bluish gray or rusty orange. It will almost always be a different color from the regular soil nearby.

The best test is to feel the clay. It should stick together and feel sticky or slippery when it is wet. Try rolling a chunk of it into a worm. If the worm holds together without completely crumbling, you have found clay.

2. Dig the clay, trying not to get ordinary soil or sand mixed in with it. Use a bucket to carry the clay.

3. Now clean the clay. To 3/4 of a bucket of clay, add water almost to the top of the bucket. Use your hands to break up lumps of clay. The object is to thoroughly mix the clay and water. Take out any large rocks or twigs.

4. After the clay and water are mixed, you will have a bucket of what is called *slip*. Place the sieve over the second bucket, and pour the slip through. The sieve will catch any large and medium-sized twigs or rocks.

5. Wash out the first bucket and the sieve. Then spread the screen on the bottom of the sieve and place sieve and screen on top of the bucket.

6. Pour the slip through the screen/sieve. This time smaller rocks and debris will be caught by the screen. The slip should be fairly smooth and clean by now. Some people stop after this step. If your slip feels smooth and clean, go on to step 9. If it still feels gritty, go to steps 7 and 8 first.

7. To get slip even cleaner, you can sieve it through cloth. Wash out the empty bucket and put it inside the old T-shirt so that a single thickness of cloth is stretched over the opening of the bucket.

8. Slowly pour the slip through the cloth. The T-shirt will droop and stretch, so pour slowly. If it droops too much, pull it tighter. You may have to add water to the slip so that it will go through the cloth. It may take a while for the slip to seep through the shirt. If the shirt becomes clogged, take it off of the bucket and rinse it.

9. Let the clean slip stand in the bucket overnight. You'll see water rising to the top after a couple of hours. Pour or scoop the water off as it rises.

10. Continue scooping and pouring until you can't get any more water off. The slip should be fairly thick.

11. Pour the thick slip onto the piece of plywood so that even more water can evaporate. Put the plywood in the sun, but be sure to cover it if it rains. Check the slip often. As soon as it is thick enough for you to make a ball out of a handful of it, roll it or scrape it off of the wood, and store it in a plastic bag. Let it sit for a couple of weeks, and it will be nicer to work with.

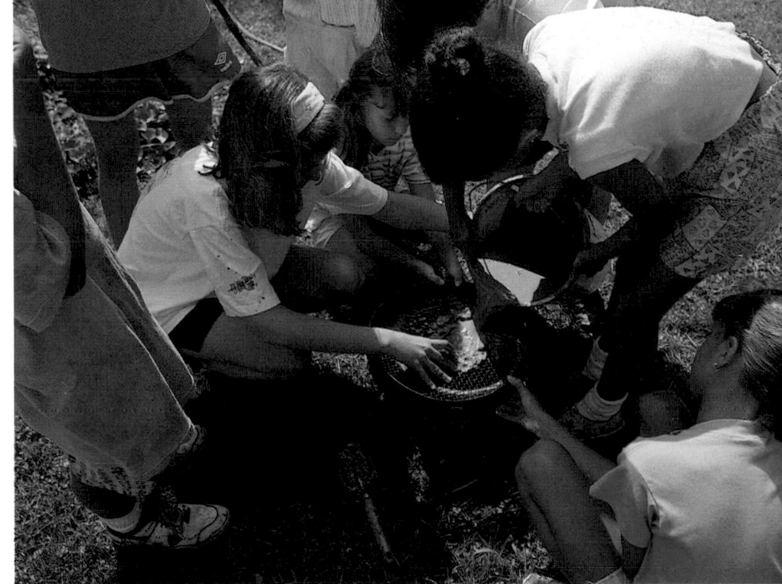

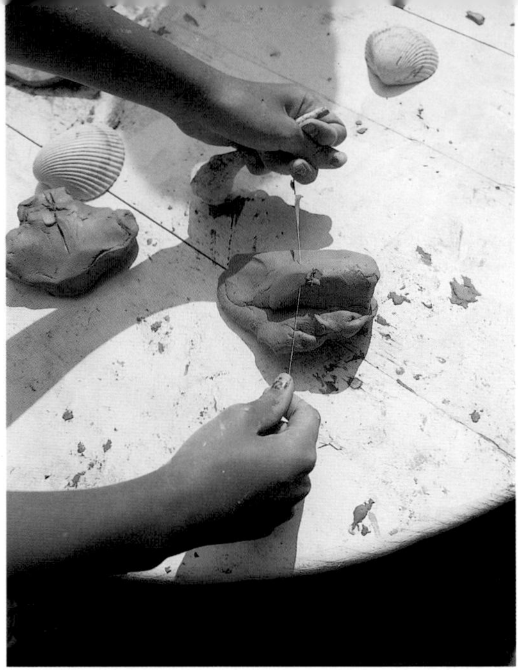

Pinch Pot

What You'll Need

- A handful of clay
- A table or countertop to work on
- A piece of monofilament about 2 feet long
- 2 sticks, each around 2 inches long, or 2 old thread spools
- Large seashells, nails, sticks, and other improvised tools for decorating pots
- A plastic bag

What to Do

1. Before making a pot, you need to *wedge* the clay in order to get rid of air bubbles that could cause it to break in the kiln. Wedge the clay by slamming it down on the table top, then pounding it, lifting it, turning it, and pounding it again. Continue pounding-lifting-turning for around 10 minutes.

2. Test the wedging this way: Tie each end of the monofilament to one of the short sticks or spools. Holding the monofilament stretched tight, use it to slice through the lump of clay.

3. Examine the two flat sides where the slice was made. They should be smooth. If they are, go on to the next step. If there are any holes or cracks, continue wedging for a few more minutes, then test again before going on.

4. Make a smooth round ball out of the clay. Wet it with a *little* water if it feels dry.

5. Push your thumb into a spot on the ball. Use your thumb to push against your other fingers as you form a bowl shape.

6. Continue pushing and stroking with your thumb and other fingers until the pot looks the way you want it to. Be careful not to pinch it too tightly or the walls may get too thin and collapse.

If the rim begins to crack, wet your finger and smooth it back together. If the opening gets too big or floppy, use a table knife to take a small slice out of the rim. Then wet your finger and smooth the two sides of the slice back together.

If you don't like the pot at all, simply roll it back into a ball, wedge it a few times, and start over.

7. When your pot looks the way you want it to, put it in a cool, dry, shady place to dry. If the weather is very hot and dry, put the pot inside an *opened* plastic bag so that it will dry slowly and evenly.

8. Check the pot the next day. It should feel cool and damp, but no longer slippery. You can now use your improvised tools to press and scratch designs into the surface of the pot. Be sure to put your fingers inside the pot to support the wall you are pressing against or it could collapse.

9. Put the decorated pot back in its drying spot. It will take a week or longer to dry completely, and it must be completely dry before you fire it. To check for dryness, hold the pot against your cheek. When it no longer feels cool, it is dry.

10. You can wait as long as you want before firing the dry pot. Just remember that unfired pottery breaks very easily. Be sure to store it on a shelf where nothing will touch or disturb it.

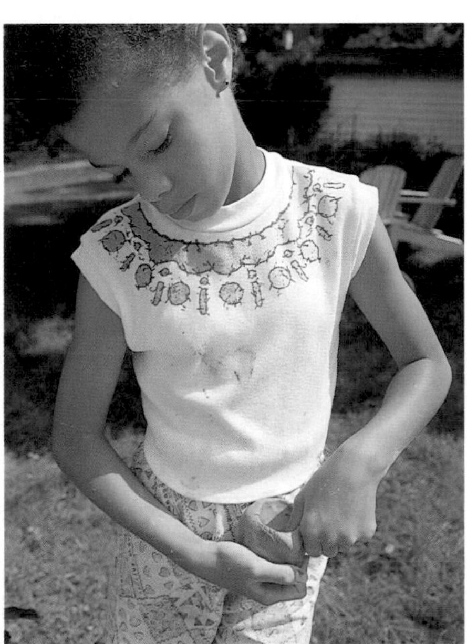

Sawdust Kiln

What You'll Need

- A metal garbage can
- A hammer
- An awl or a large nail
- A large screwdriver
- Bricks or stones to put under the kiln
- A garbage bag full of DRY sawdust
- Old newspapers
- Matches
- 3 small wads of clay
- Old newspapers
- A bucket of water

What to Do

1. Using the hammer and the awl or nail, punch a row of 3 holes on 4 sides of the can. Use the screwdriver to enlarge the holes until they are at least 1/2 inch across.

2. Place the bricks or stones on the ground for the kiln to stand on. It's best to put the kiln on ground that has no grass growing on it and to clear away any dry leaves or other things that could easily catch fire. Keep the bucket of water nearby in case of emergency.

3. Put 4 inches of dry sawdust in the bottom of the kiln.

4. Carefully place the first layer of pots, leaving 2 to 3 inches between each pot and 4 inches between the pots and the kiln walls. If you are using a small can, you may be able to fit only one pot in each layer. Fill the insides of the pots with sawdust, and remove the lids.

5. Cover the pots with 3 to 4 inches of sawdust, and place another layer.

6. Keep layering pots until you get to the top 6 inches of the can. Then put 2 inches of sawdust, and finish off with twists of newspaper. To make a twist of newspaper, pleat half a sheet of newspaper. Then twist the folded paper starting at the center.

7. Place twists of newspaper side by side to fill the top layer of the kiln.

8. Put 3 small wads of clay equal distances apart on the rim of the can. These will hold the lid up enough to vent the fire and let it breathe.

9. Light the newspaper. Once the twists have caught fire, rest the lid on the clay wads to cover the kiln.

10. Check the fire often until it is going smoothly. Make sure the sawdust lights after the newspaper fire burns out. If the sawdust stops burning, add more newspaper and light the fire again. You should not see flames once the newspaper goes out, but the top layer of sawdust should look all black, and you should see heat waves and smoke coming out from under the cover. If the sawdust burns too fast, add more sawdust to smother it and slow it down. If it still burns too fast, spray a little water on it.

What you are aiming for is a slow, even smoldering that burns from top to bottom. Sometimes it takes several tries to get the kiln to burn evenly.

11. There is very little danger of fire from a metal can

kiln. Keep the cover on when you aren't around, and you can leave it for hours at a time and even overnight. Post a sign a few feet away from it, warning people not to touch it.

12. After 24 hours or longer, when smoke no longer comes from under the lid or from the vent holes, open the kiln. The sawdust should be black, and the top layer of pots should be visible. Let the pots cool (which may take several more hours), then carefully remove them. Brush off any remaining sawdust.

13. Pots fired in a sawdust kiln are not waterproof. They are also rather easily broken, although they are certainly stronger than they were before being fired. Rub the pots with a soft rag to bring out the black, gray, or white shine. These pots will have a mysterious, primitive look.

Wild Flower Candles

What You'll Need

- Paraffin
- Fat white candles
- Pressed wild flowers
- An old tin can with label removed
- An old soft paintbrush
- A pot of water
- Old newspapers

What to Do

1. Collect some wild flowers and press them. Put the flowers between two sheets of paper towel and stack a big book on top, or use a flower press. They'll need to dry for several days.
2. On the day of the project, gather your materials. Be sure the flowers are flat and rather dry.
3. Ask a grownup to help you melt a few chunks of paraffin. To do this, put water in the pot and put the paraffin in the can. Put the can of paraffin in the water. Boil the water in the pot. Watch the paraffin carefully, for it can catch fire easily. *Never melt paraffin directly over the burner. Always use the double boiler method described above.*
4. Hold a candle in one hand so that one side of it is level, and place a wild flower on the candle.
5. Dip the paintbrush in the melted paraffin.
6. Quickly but carefully brush a thin layer of paraffin over the flower to glue it to the side of the candle. If your paintbrush hardens, dip it in the warm paraffin.
7. Continue placing the flowers and painting them down. The paraffin will cool quickly and will harden as it cools.

DRYING LEAVES AND FLOWERS

Many of the interesting plants you find on nature walks and in your yard can be saved by drying them. When you dry a flower or herb, you are actually removing the natural moisture that all plants have in their petals, leaves, and stems. As the moisture leaves, you may notice some changes. Sometimes the petals shrivel up and turn brown. Other times the petals get a bit smaller and turn a lighter color. And sometimes, in what seems like a miracle, a dried flower looks exactly like a fresh-picked one.

Be sure to cut the flowers you want to dry on a sunny morning after the dew has dried and to check on the drying flowers every three to four days. The petals and leaves of a dried plant feel like a crisp sheet of paper.

Hang-Drying

Arrange the flowers in small bundles of three to five stems. Tie each bundle together around the stems with sewing thread or string and hang them upside down in a dark place that's not too damp. (Be sure you check the flowers for tiny bugs before you bring them inside!)

Desiccant-Drying

Desiccants are substances like cat litter, borax, and sand that can absorb moisture. Put a layer of desiccant into a card-board box, and then add the flowers. Allow a little bit of space between the flowers. Cover the flowers with another layer of desiccant and keep the top on the box while they're drying.

PRESSING LEAVES AND FLOWERS

For some craft projects, like gift tags and candles, you want leaves and flowers that are flat as well as dry. Pressing them will make them nice and flat.

The easiest way to press materials is to lay them on a paper towel, cover them with another paper towel, and stack a heavy book on top. If you leave them for several days to a week, they should emerge dry and flat—ready to decorate lots of different things.

Gift Tags, Book Marks, Note Cards

What You'll Need

- Construction paper
- A pencil
- A ruler
- Pressed leaves and flowers
- A small, pointed paint brush
- White glue
- Crayons, paint pens, or pastel crayons
- Clear self-sticking plastic with removable backing*

*Available at most department stores and discount marts.

What to Do

1. Using the pencil and ruler, draw the outline of your bookmark, tag, or card on the construction paper. If you're making gift tags (as shown in the photo) or note cards, make them big enough to fold in half, and decorate only the front half.
2. Lay your pressed flowers and leaves on the tag, in a pattern you like. Move them carefully, for they are delicate and will break. (A dry paint brush is good for moving them around.)
3. When you get the pressed materials where you want them, pick up one large piece at a time, and use the paint brush to put a *little* white glue on the back. Then put the piece back into position. You only need to glue the large parts, not the stems or tiny leaves.
4. Once everything is glued in place and has had time to dry, look at the design and decide if it needs more decoration. If it does, use your crayons, paint pens, or pastels to add lines or whatever you want. Be careful not to disturb the pressed leaves and flowers.
5. Cut out a piece of contact plastic larger than the outline of the gift tag. Peel off the backing and place the plastic over the tag. Starting at one end, smooth down the plastic and press it firmly against your design.
6. Cut out the gift tag.

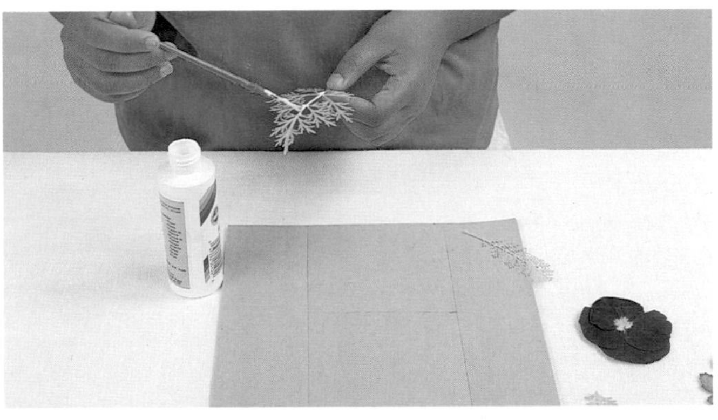

Candied Violets

Violets bloom in the early spring, telling us that winter is really over. They grow in damp, shady places and may be white, yellow, or pale lavender, but their best-known color is, of course, "violet." Their heart-shaped leaves and five-petaled flowers are used in soups and salads, and both can be "candied"—although candied leaves are mostly for decoration. Candied flowers look nice on top of cake, fruit, or ice cream.

What You'll Need

- Violet flowers and leaves
- An egg white
- Sugar
- Brushes

What to Do

1. Wash the violets and leaves, and let them dry.
2. Separate the egg. To do that, hold it over a small, clean bowl, and crack the shell about in the middle. Then pour the egg back and forth between the two shell halves, keeping the yolk in the shell and letting the white run into the bowl. Throw away the shell and the yolk.
3. Dip the small brush in the egg white, and brush it on the violet petals, covering both the front and back sides.
4. Sprinkle sugar on the violets, covering them completely.
5. Put the violets on waxed paper to dry.
6. You can candy the leaves the same way.

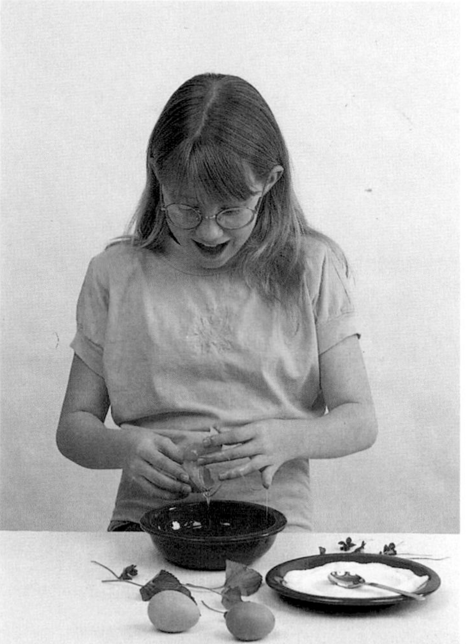

Wormery

What You'll Need

- A quart-sized glass jar
- Sand
- Dark garden soil
- A trowel
- Worms
- Rotted leaves/compost
- A spray bottle of water
- Black construction paper big enough to wrap around the jar
- Cellophane tape
- Scissors
- Squeeze-on plastic fabric paints

What to Do

1. Place a layer of sand around 1-1/2 inches deep in the jar.
2. Place a layer of soil around the same depth on top of the sand.
3. Continue alternating layers of sand and soil, smoothing each layer as you go.
4. Add 3 or 4 earthworms to the top layer of soil.
5. Cover the top layer with a layer of rotted leaves or compost.
6. Spray the compost or leaves lightly with water.
7. Cut black paper to fit around the jar.
8. Put a strip of tape down one short edge of the paper, about an inch from the end.
9. Decorate the paper with squeeze-on plastic paint.
10. Wrap the paper around the jar end. Make a tab of tape that is attached to the paper on the end that does not have the strip of tape. When the paper is wrapped, you can stick and unstick the tape tab to the shiny cellophane tape strip.
11. Untape the tab after a few days and remove the paper to see what the worms have done to the layers of sand and soil. Make a drawing of their tunnels every few days to record their actions.

EAT DIRT, YOU WORM!

Worms don't just push their way through the soil, they *eat* their way through. In a single day an earthworm gobbles up more than its own weight in dirt, sand, bits of leaves and grass, and almost anything else that happens to be in its way as it burrows from one place to another. By the time the stuff comes out the worm's other end, it has been ground up and mixed with the worm's own body fluids and is a perfect food for plants. (That's why gardeners are always so happy to find earthworms in their garden.)

Sometimes you see worm castings, like little piled-up mud pies, on the ground. But most castings are left behind in the ground, where they become part of the soil.

Earthworms also get food by coming to the surface at night and pulling leaves and other pieces of plants into their burrows. In one study of earthworms in an apple orchard, scientists discovered that, by spring, night crawlers had buried 90% of all the leaves that had fallen the year before—about a ton of leaves per acre!

Worms, in fact, are the reason why Roman ruins

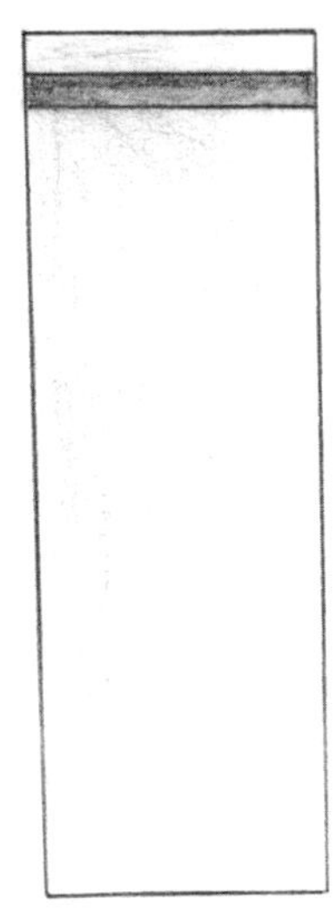

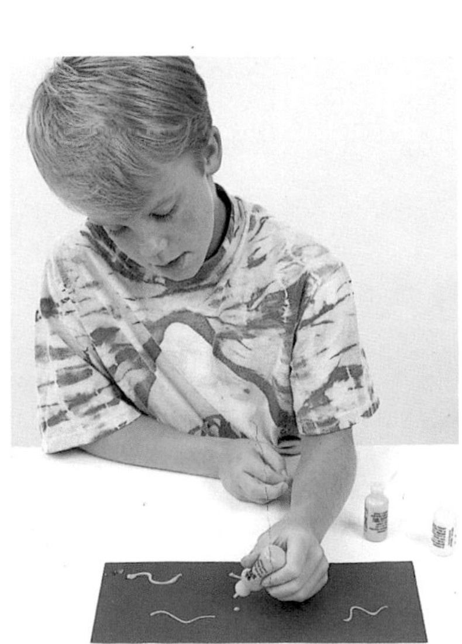

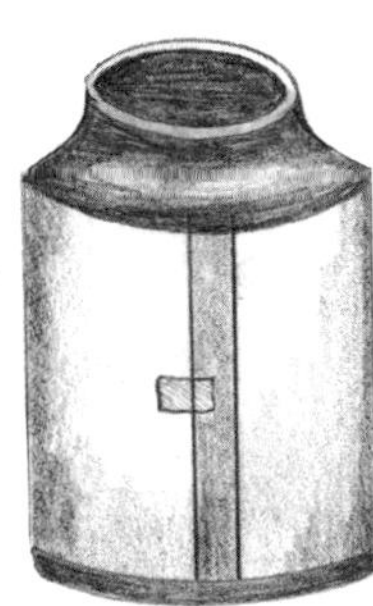

and other ancient buildings seem to "sink" into the ground over the centuries. By constantly churning up the dirt beneath the foundations and adding new soil near the surface, worms gradually bury the buildings.

The reason why earthworms can do so much is that there are so many of them. Researchers have counted as many as two *million* earthworms per acre in some soils in the United States. That's more than 400 worms in every square yard. In fact, the worms in an acre of rich pasture may weigh more than the cows and horses grazing on it—as much as 12 tons!

No wonder earthworms make so much good topsoil. Scientists say that, on the average, the earthworms in an acre of ground add 105,000 pounds of castings to the soil every year!

SUMMER

Sun Prints

What You'll Need

You'll need to buy two things at a camera shop:

- A package of photographic paper, either 5 x 7 inches or larger
- A package of fixer (sodium thiosulfate)

You'll also need:

- A piece of glass slightly larger than the photographic paper
- A piece of heavy cardboard slightly larger than the glass
- A glass dish about 10 x 6 x 2 inches (a glass baking dish would do nicely)
- A sink
- A flat counter top
- Grasses, ferns, feathers, seed heads—whatever you would like to print

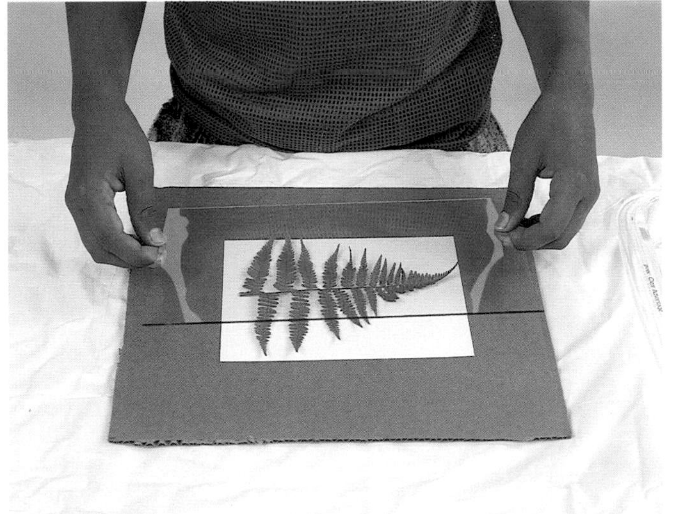

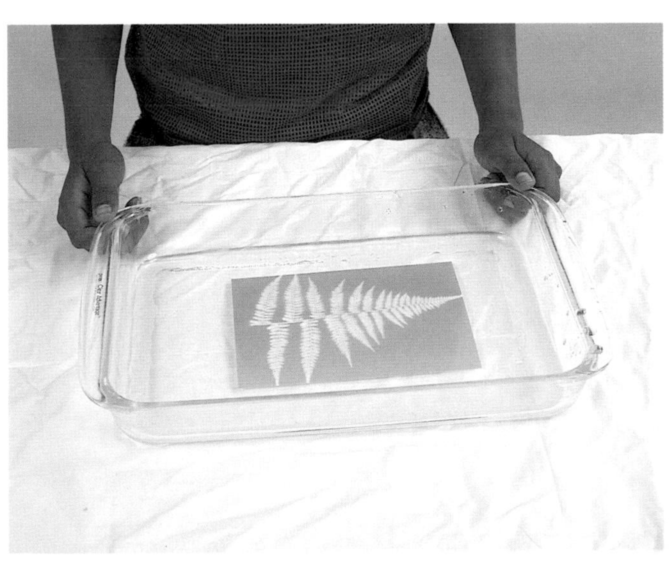

What to Do

1. Clean the glass and the glass dish, and dry them both.
2. Put 2 cups of warm water in the glass dish.
3. Slowly add 1/4 cup of fixer crystals to the water, stirring as you add.
4. Take one sheet of photographic paper out of its black, light-proof envelope and lay it on the cardboard, shiny side up.
5. Arrange the items you are printing on the paper. For example, if you're printing a fern, lay it on the paper.
6. Cover the paper and the items with the piece of glass.
7. Put the cardboard with paper and glass in bright sunlight for about 100 seconds. The paper will turn grayish purple.
8. Bring everything inside. (If the paper begins to get pink in places, bring it inside even if the 100 seconds aren't up.)
9. Carefully remove the glass and the items that were printed, and place the paper in the fixer solution. Stir the fixer around and over the print for around 2 minutes. Try not to touch the surface of the print. If it starts to get faded, take it out of the fixer and go on to the next step, even if the two minutes aren't up yet.
10. Rinse the print under cool running water for about 5 minutes.
11. Lay the print on a flat surface to dry. You can use the counter top. The print will change color as it dries.
12. You can punch holes in your prints and tie them together with yarn to make a collection. Or you might want to glue them with rubber cement to colored paper and hang them up for display.

Sun Clock

What You'll Need

- A saw
- A piece of wood about 12 inches square
- A piece of plywood or hardboard 1/8 inch thick and about 6 inches by 8 inches
- Two 6-inch strips of wooden molding
- Carpenter's glue
- A watch with hands
- A pencil
- Acrylic paints
- A paintbrush
- Urethane varnish
- A varnish brush

What to Do

1. Cut the wood into the shapes shown in the drawing.
2. Stand the blade up as shown in the picture, exactly in the middle along one edge of the square board. Glue the blade to the board, and glue the pieces of molding on both sides of the blade.
3. Place the sundial in a spot that gets sun all day long. You could put it on the ground, on a tree stump, on a concrete block, or on a few bricks. Wherever it is, place the sundial so that the blade points to the north. Step 4 will tell you how to find north.
4. On a sunny day, hold your watch in your hand and turn it so the hour hand points to the sun. Holding the watch very still, find the spot exactly between the hour hand and the 12. That spot points

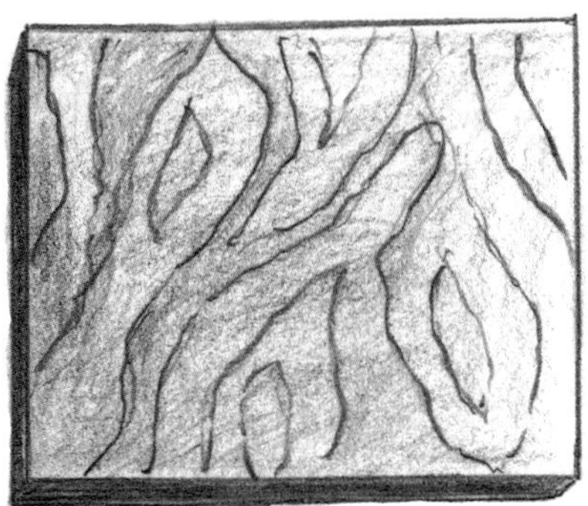

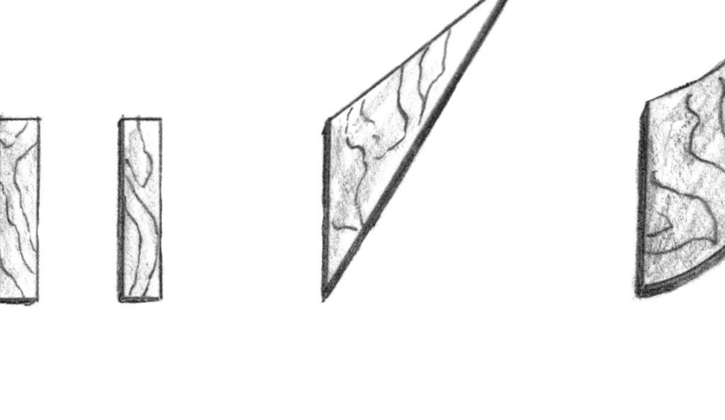

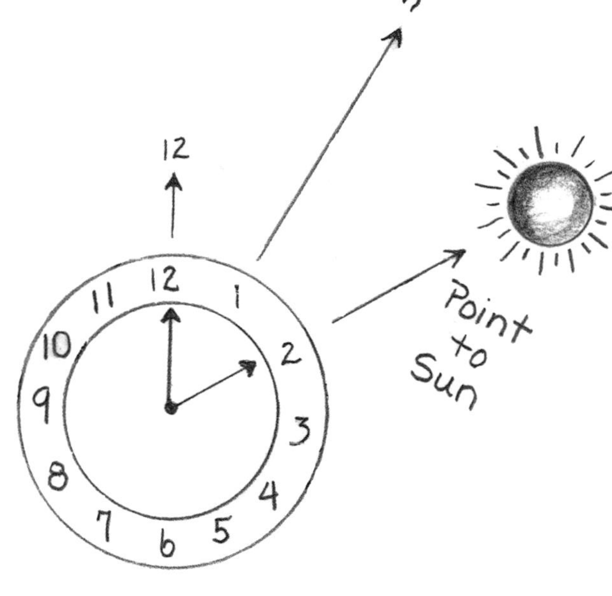

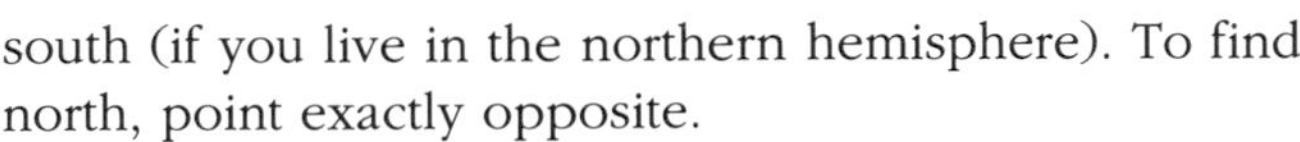

south (if you live in the northern hemisphere). To find north, point exactly opposite.

5. Turn your sun clock so that the blade points north. Mark the position of the clock so you can return it to the same position if you need to move it.

6. This step may take a couple of days. Go outside every hour on the hour, and use a pencil to draw the shadow of the blade on the sundial. Be sure to mark the time on the clock also.

7. After you've marked all the hours of daylight, paint the sun clock. Be sure to include the numerals so you can read them as the shadow of the blade moves across the face of the dial. (We've used Roman numerals, but you can use regular numerals if you'd rather.)

8. With a paint brush, coat the entire sun clock, back and front, with urethane varnish to weatherproof it.

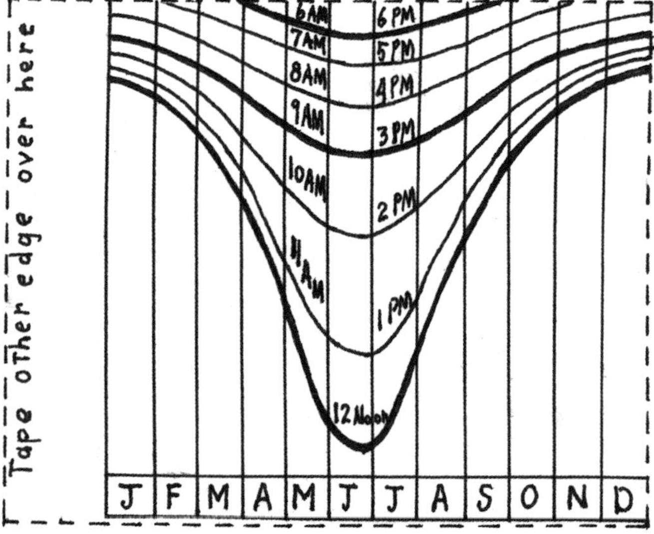

Pocket Sundial

The sundial is the oldest scientific instrument still in use. Long before mechanical clocks and watches were invented, people used sundials to tell time.

As the sun moves across the sky, the shadows it casts change their position. Ancient peoples learned to mark where shadows fell on a sundial to tell the time of day.

This particular sundial is called a cylinder, or shepherd's dial. It was widely used hundreds of years ago because it was inexpensive, simple to make, and easy to carry. Some dials were more elaborate. George Washington carried a silver pocket dial.

What You'll Need

- A wooded dowel 1 inch thick (a piece of broomstick would do)
- A nail or an awl
- A screw eye
- A wire nail 1 inch long
- A saw
- A hammer

What to Do

1. Cut a piece of dowel 4 inches long.
2. With a nail or awl, make a small hole in the top of the dowel, and screw the screw eye into it. The screw eye must be in the center of the dowel end.
3. Hammer the wire nail lightly into the dowel about 1/2 inch from the top (the end with the screw eye). Drive the nail in only far enough to hold it firmly. Be sure the nail sticks straight out.
4. Use a photocopy machine to copy the sundial graph, and carefully cut it out along the dotted lines. Also cut out the small dotted circle. You can color the hour lines if you like.
5. Wrap the graph around the dowel, with the top touching the nail.
6. Overlap the ends of the graph, and tape it with cellophane tape. Don't let the tape touch the dial. Leave the graph a little loose so it can turn freely on the dowel.
7. Push the graph up until it touches the nail, and place a thumbtack at the bottom of the graph to keep it from sliding back down. Don't put the tack through the graph (the graph must turn).
8. Tie a short piece of string to the screw eye.
9. Glue the small circle that you cut out to the bottom end of sundial.

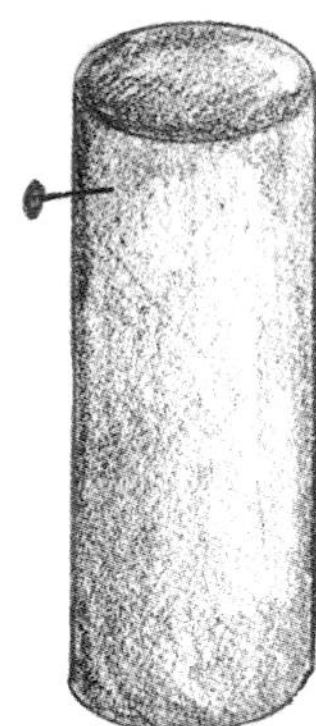

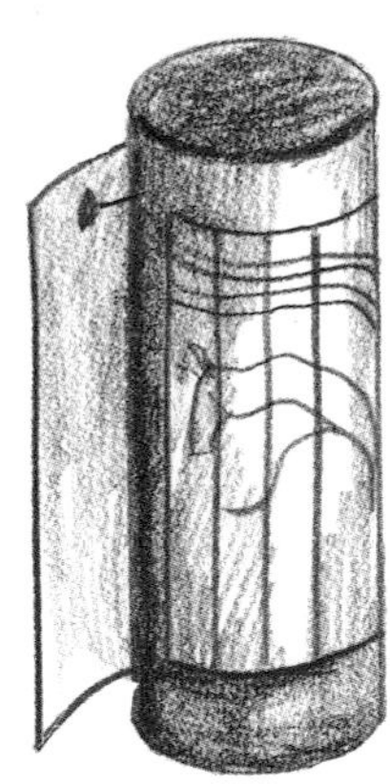

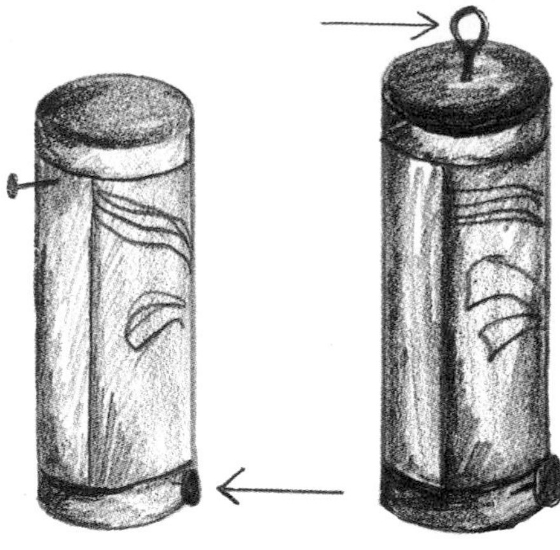

HOW TO USE YOUR SUNDIAL

1. The letters at the bottom of the graph represent the months of the year. Turn the graph on the dowel until the letter for the current month is directly below the nail.

2. Stand with your back to the sun and hold your dial up by the string. (The sun must be shining for the dial to work.)

3. Slowly rotate the entire dial until the shadow of the nail points straight down.

4. The shadow of the head of the nail will indicate the time on the graph. Notice where this nailhead shadow falls on the graph. Each curved line on the graph stands for two different hours. For example, 9 a.m. and 3 p.m. share the same line. If the shadow falls here it is either 9 a.m. or 3 p.m. You must decide which time it really is. Note: During Daylight Savings Time you will have to add one hour to the reading to get the correct time.

5. *Important:* Until you adjust the dial for your location it will not read correctly.

HOW TO ADJUST YOUR SUNDIAL

1. Hold the dial up in the sunlight and see where the nailhead shadow falls. Read the time on the graph.

2. Now, read the time on a normal clock or watch. You must adjust the length of the nail until your dial reads the same time as the clock. You can do this by slowly hammering the nail in until the dial reads correctly, or you may cut the nail off until it is correct.

3. *Important:* If you are doing this during Daylight Savings Time you must adjust the nail to read one hour less than what the clock reads. Later, when using the sundial, you must add one hour to the reading to get the correct time.

Leaf Print

What You'll Need

- Paper
- A pencil
- A plate
- Fresh leaves and/or flowers
- A paint brush about 1 inch wide
- Poster or tempera paints
- Box of tissues

What to Do

1. On an extra piece of paper, arrange your leaves and flowers in a circle, to get an idea of what you would like to make with them.

2. Using a pencil, lightly draw a circle on the paper you're going to use for your print. You can make the circle round by tracing around a plate.

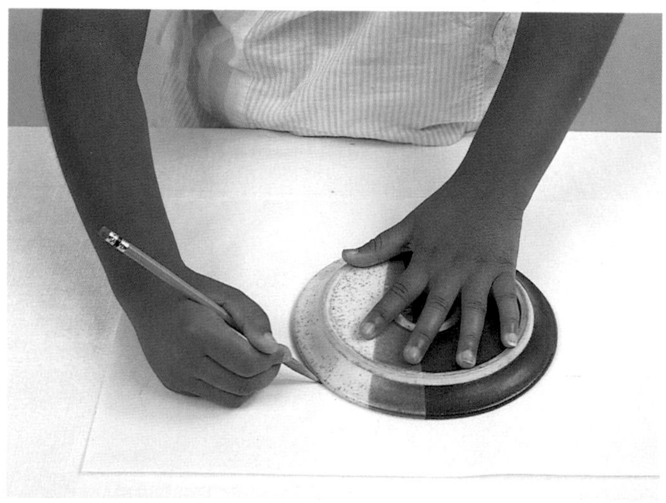

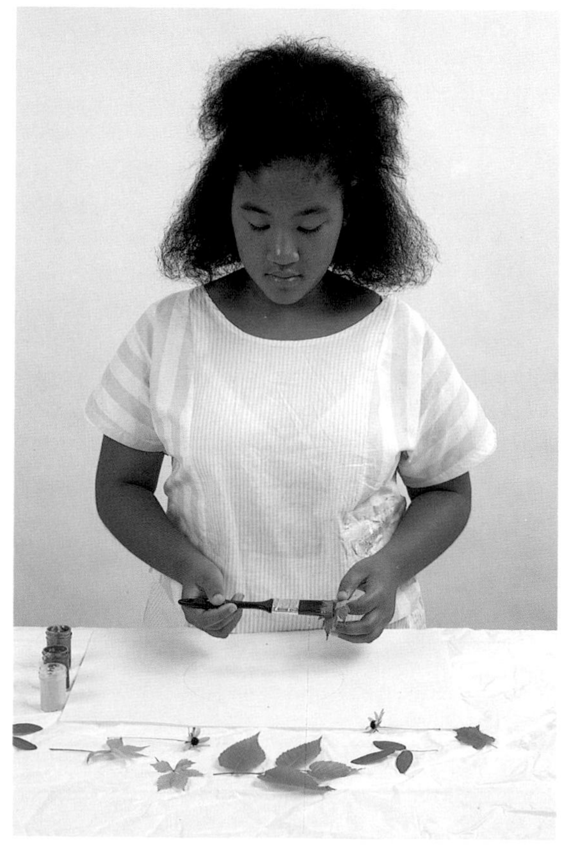

3. Make a dot on the circle at the top center and the bottom center.

4. Brush paint on the back of a leaf, and place it carefully on the circle you've drawn. Make sure not to move it around, or the paint will smudge. (If you like, you can practice first on scrap paper.)

5. Cover the leaf with a tissue and smooth it down lightly. After a few seconds, lift the tissue and gently peel off the leaf.

6. Repeat the process with other leaves and flowers, working your way down one side of the circle and then the other.

WHICH LEAF IS WHICH?

There are over 330,000 different kinds of leafy plants in the world—and every one of them has its own special type of leaf!

For instance, some plants have leaves with *saw-toothed edges,* while others have perfectly *smooth* edges.

Saw-toothed vs. smooth.

Some plants' leaves grow directly across the branch from another leaf. Those are known as *opposite-leaved plants.* Other plants have leaves that are never opposite each other. Instead, first there's a leaf on the left, then one on the right, then the next is on the left, and so on. Those are known as *alternate-leaved plants.*

Opposite vs. alternate.

Another clue is the number of leaflets or leaf blades—the flat green part—attached to the stem. *Simple* leaves have just one blade. *Compound* leaves have three or more leaflets on the same stem. *Hand-shaped* compound leaves have leaflets that are arranged like your fingers when you spread out your hand, or like the spokes of a wheel. *Feather-shaped* compound leaves have leaflets arranged up and down both sides of the stem, so the whole thing looks like a big feather.

Of course, leaves aren't just shapes and patterns. Each has its own special beauty. Some leaves are a slightly different color on top than on the bottom. Some reflect the sun's light more intensely than others. And have you noticed that each kind of leaf has its own way of moving in the breeze, depending on its shape, the length or stiffness of its stem, and the way it's attached to the branch? Oak leaves wave up and down, hickory leaves sway and bob, aspen leaves flutter like butterfly wings.

Simple vs. compound.

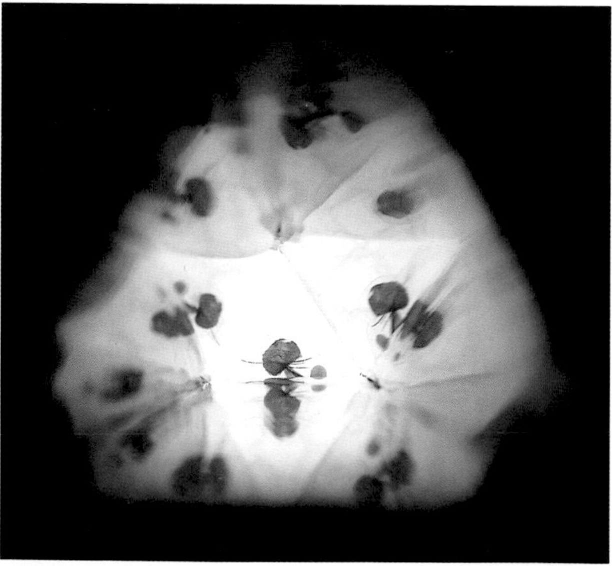

Nature Kaleidoscope

This project is more complicated than some others in this book, but not as hard as it might look at first. And when you're done, you'll have a kaleidoscope different from anyone else's. Hold it to the light, look through the eyehole, and watch beautiful patterns and colors take shape.

What You'll Need

- A small (4-inch or 10-inch) mailing tube with a lid that slides off and on*
- A sharp craft knife
- A pencil
- A hammer

- An awl
- A large screwdriver
- A ruler
- A piece of light cardboard (such as the lid of a shoe box) at least 6 inches wide and as long as your mailing tube
- A sheet of clear acetate**
- A fat permanent black marker that will write on acetate
- Clear contact paper
- Pressed flowers, leaves, and stems

*Look for mailing tubes where stationery and mailing labels are sold.
**Clear acetate is sold in art supply stores.

What to Do

1. Take the cap off the mailing tube. Use the craft knife to cut the metal end off the cap.
2. Cut a 1/2-inch-wide cylinder off the end of the mailing tube. (To make sure your cut is even, mark dots 1/2 inch from the end of the tube in 4 or 5 places, then connect the dots. Use the line to guide you as you cut.)
3. Now make your eyehole. Use the hammer and awl to punch several holes as close together as possible in the metal end of the mailing tube. Then use the screwdriver to ream out the nail holes until you've got one hole about 1/4 inch across.

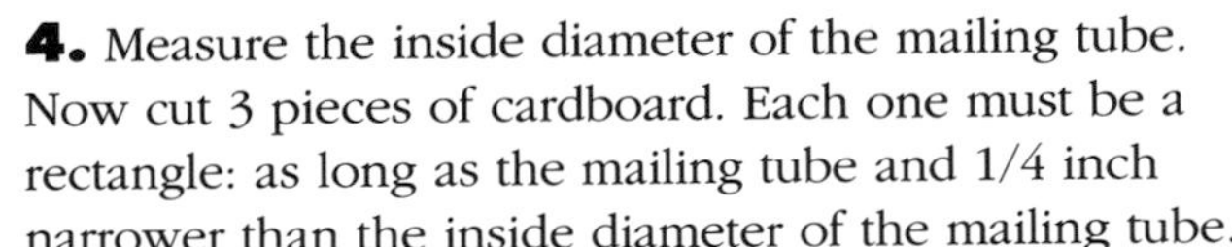

4. Measure the inside diameter of the mailing tube. Now cut 3 pieces of cardboard. Each one must be a rectangle: as long as the mailing tube and 1/4 inch narrower than the inside diameter of the mailing tube.
5. Cut 3 pieces of acetate the exact size as the 3 pieces of cardboard.
6. Use the marker to completely blacken one side of each piece of acetate.
7. Tape a piece of acetate to each piece of cardboard, with the blackened side against the cardboard. Put the tape only along the short edges of the cardboard, and bend the piece of tape over the end to make it stay.
8. Tape the 3 pieces of cardboard into a 3-sided triangular shape, with the black sides facing inside.
9. Carefully slide the cardboard triangle into the mailing tube, pushing it all the way to the end. The end of the triangle should be even with the rim of the tube. If it sticks out, take it out and trim it to fit. And it should fit tightly into the tube. If it's loose, put tape around the outside to pad it.
10. Next make the endpiece. Use the 1/2-inch cylinder (the one you cut off the mailing tube) to draw one circle on acetate and one on a piece of clear contact paper that has been folded over and stuck together to make a double sheet. Cut out both circles.
11. Tape the acetate circle over one end of the 1/2-inch cylinder.
12. Peel the backing from a piece of clear contact

Mailing tube

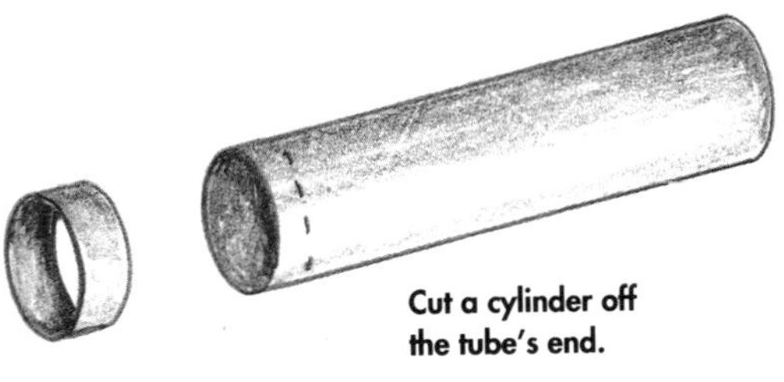

Cut a cylinder off the tube's end.

Cut metal end off cap

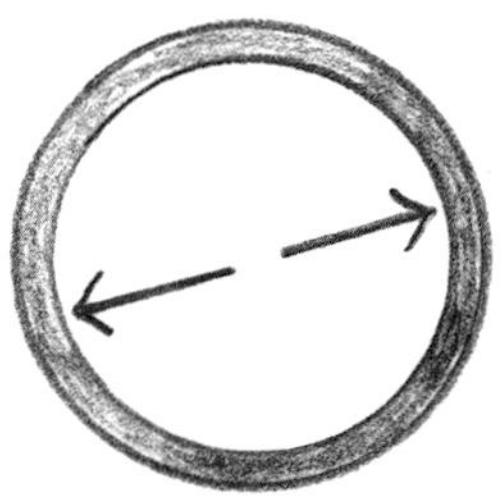

Measure inside diameter.

Cut 3 pieces of cardboard and 3 of acetate.

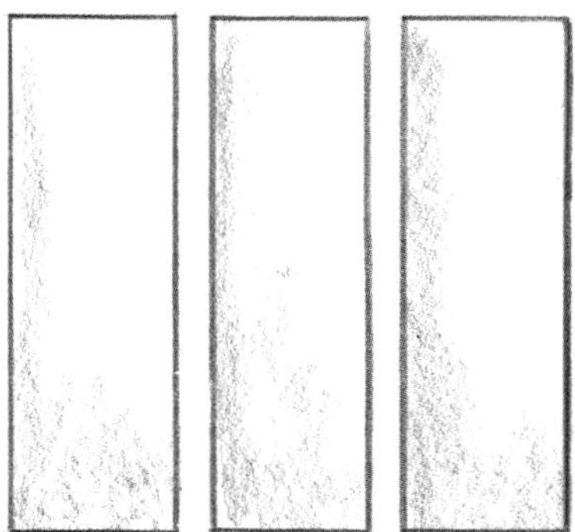

Tape acetate to cardboard

Tape cardboard pieces to form triangle

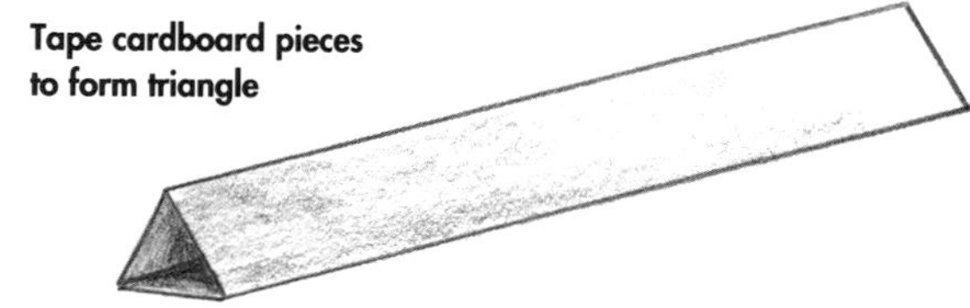

Insert triangle into mailing tube

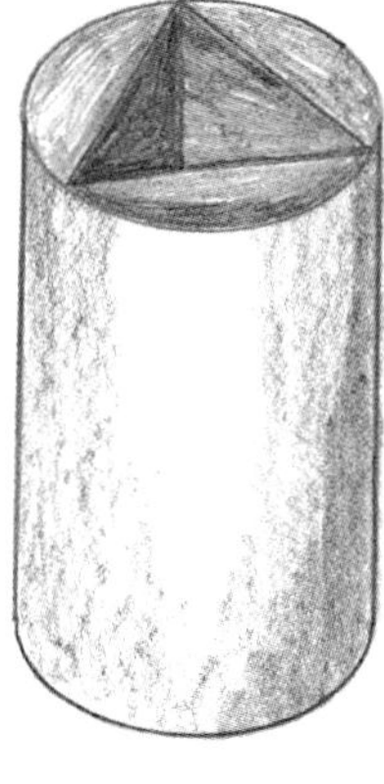

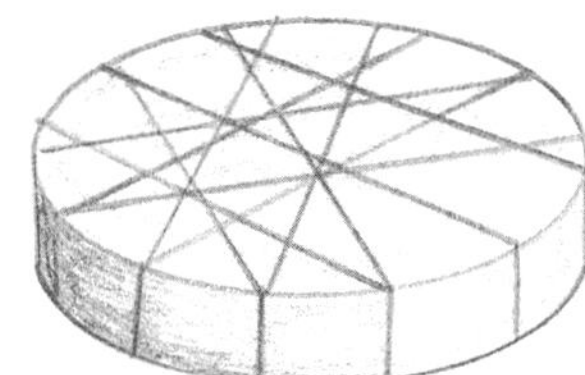

Make endpiece

Insert endpiece into tube

paper that is about 8 inches by 8 inches square. Place it sticky-side-up on the table. Carefully lay pressed flowers, small leaves, and small stems on the contact paper, with about an inch of empty paper around each leaf and flower. Now cover each leaf and flower with clear cellophane tape. Cut out the leaves and flowers and place them in the cylinder. Be sure there are no sticky edges. If the pieces seem to be clumping together, check again for sticky edges.

13. Tape the double-layered contact-paper circle over the open end of the cylinder, just as you taped the acetate circle over the other end. Shake it gently to be sure the pieces inside can move about freely.

14. Carefully slide the endpiece (the taped cylinder) into one end of the cap. Adjust the endpiece until it's even with the edge of the cap.

15. Put the cap (with the endpiece inside) onto the mailing tube. At this point you can test your kaleidoscope by looking toward a window and gently turning the cap while holding the mailing tube up to your eye. Try looking at different sources of light—a window, a light bulb.

16. To decorate the outside of your kaleidoscope, cut a piece of contact paper the same height as the part of the tube you want to decorate, and wide enough to wrap around it. Peel the backing off the paper, and lay pressed leaves or flowers on the sticky paper. Then carefully wrap the paper around the tube, smoothing out any bubbles as you wrap. Or you could draw designs on the tube, or glue cut-out pictures from magazines all over the outside of the tube with rubber cement.

WHAT DO LEAVES DO?

Have you ever leaned back under a shade tree and watched the leaves above you flutter in the breeze? You'd never guess that each one of those leaves is an amazing chemical factory. Leaves manufacture their own food by capturing energy from the sun and using it, in a process called photosynthesis, to change water from the soil and carbon dioxide gas from the air into simple sugar. At the same time, leaves release water vapor and oxygen (the gas we humans need to breathe) into the air.

Fortunately, leaves make much more food than they need for their own growth. They store the leftovers as starches, fats, oils, proteins, and other nutrients. When people or animals or insects eat the plants (or when they eat other creatures that have eaten the plants), they get that stored nourishment. Leaves, in other words, are the planet's basic food factories. Without them, there would be no life on Earth.

The water vapor that leaves give off is also vital. Plants take water in through their roots and draw it up to their leaves for photosynthesis. Most of the water, though, isn't needed, and evaporates into the air through tiny holes, called stomata, in leaf tissue. Stomata are like the pores in human skin, only much smaller. There are about 161,000 stomata in just one square inch of an apple leaf!

Leaves release so much moisture into the air that they affect humidity and rainfall patterns. An average-size birch tree has about 200,000 leaves and releases more than 4,500 gallons of water in a single summer. The blades of grass in an acre of lawn give off 27,000 gallons of water every week during the growing season! According to some estimates, leaves are responsible for more than half of all the water that falls as rain on the Amazon rain forest!

THE BIGGEST

■ The world's largest leaves are 65 feet long, with stems up to 13 feet. They grow on two kinds of palm trees: the raffia palm, which grows in the Masearene Islands in the Indian Ocean, and the Amazonian bamboo palm, which is native to South America.

■ The world's largest floating leaf is that of the Royal water lily *(Victoria amazonica)*. The huge, platelike discs grow up to 8 feet in diameter and will support a 50-pound child.

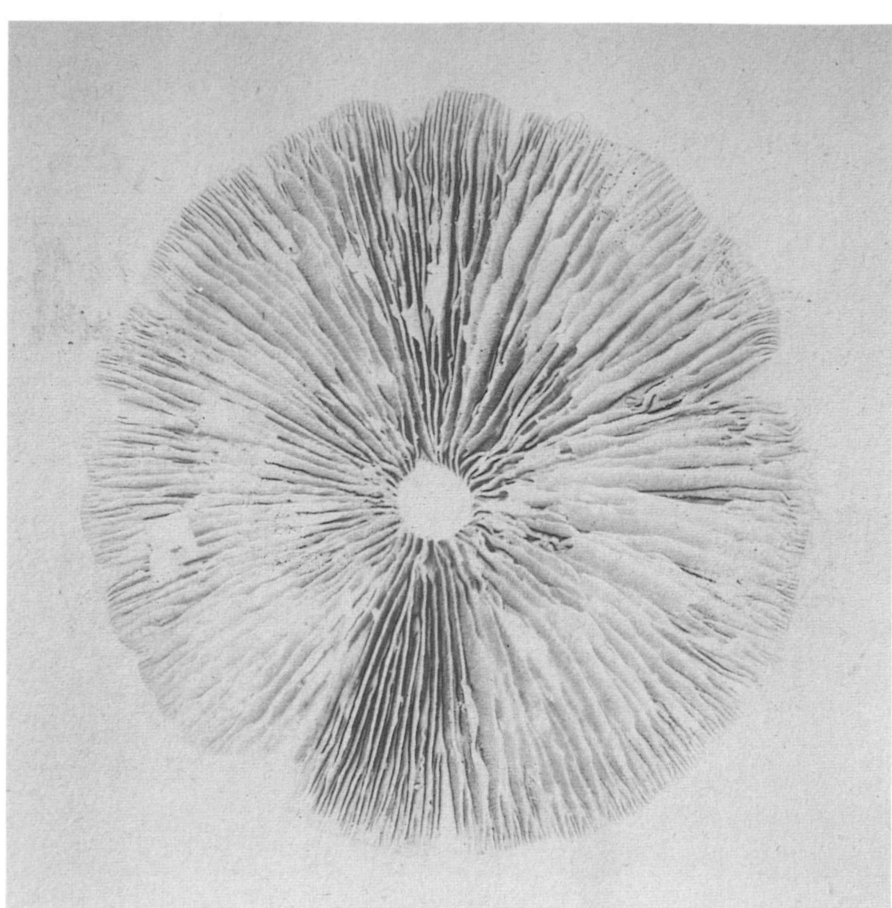

Mushroom Spore Prints

Mushrooms come in various colors, and so do the spores they make. By catching the spores on paper before they have a chance to be spread around by the wind, you can make colorful mushroom "fingerprints."

What You'll Need

- Construction paper
- Fresh round-capped mushrooms
- A sharp knife or single-edge razor blade (BE CAREFUL!)
- Bowls or jars big enough to cover the mushroom caps
- A can of hair spray or artist's fixative
- A place to work away from breezes or drafts

Mysterious Mushrooms

Imagine an apple tree that grows entirely under the ground. The trunk and branches are buried. The only time you know the tree is there at all is when the apples pop up out of the soil, one at a time or in little bunches.

Of course, apples don't grow that way. But mushrooms do. A mushroom is the fruit of a plant with "branches" that grow underground, or in any sort of rotting stuff such as old wood or layers of leaves. Next time you find a mushroom, dig around it and you'll discover the "tree": a bunch of fine white threads all tangled together, called mycelium ("my-SEAL-ee-um"). The threads themselves are the "branches," and are called hyphae (HI-fee).

The mushroom's main purpose in life is to make spores. Spores are tiny "seeds" that will grow new mushroom plants. Even big spores are no larger than a speck of dust.

Most mushrooms have a stem and a cap. If you turn the cap over, you'll probably find a circle of thin, fleshy gills or hundreds of little holes. That's where the spores are—millions of them, waiting for a breeze to blow them into the air. Different kinds of mushrooms have different colors of spores. Sometimes, if you run your finger across the gills or holes, you can see a fine powder of spores on your skin. Or, you can take a spore print to see what color the "seeds" are.

What to Do

1. Cut off each mushroom's stem where it's attached to the cap.

2. Put the caps gill-side-down on construction paper. Try using different colors of paper to make the spore prints stand out. If the mushroom's gills are brown, gray, or black, use yellow or white paper. If the gills are white, use green, red, or some other bright color.

3. Put a bowl or jar over each cap to keep drafts out. Leave the mushrooms covered overnight.

4. The next morning, carefully lift the caps straight up off the paper. You'll find an interesting, round spore print under each one. The gills make a circular pattern, like a windmill or the spokes of a wheel.

5. Use hair spray or fixative to keep the spore prints from smudging. Be careful, though, or the spray will blow the spores. Hold the can about one foot away from and above the paper, and aim straight out (not down) at the print, so the spray falls gently on the print. Let the print dry, then spray it one or two more times to make sure it's completely protected.

All mushrooms make spores, but not all have a stem, or even a cap. If you see a soft white or gray ball growing on the ground, you've found a puffball mushroom. Give it a gentle poke with your finger. Poof! Out comes a cloud of spores, like a puff of smoke.

In fact, there are thousands of kinds of mushrooms, in all sorts of shapes and colors. No wonder people have always thought mushrooms are magical and mysterious! There are mushrooms that look like icicles, turkey tails, sponges, trumpets, bowls, and pig's ears. There are green, orange, yellow, purple, bright red, and yellow mushrooms. Some ooze a milky liquid when you touch them. Others bruise blue or red. A few even glow in the dark!

Mushrooms have interesting names, too: shaggy mane, black jellydrops, witch's hat, hen of the woods, bear's head, beefsteak, stinkhorn, man-on-a-horse, and prince. Poisonous mushrooms have scary names, like panther cap, death cap, and destroying angel.

Because there are so many different types, and because they're so easy to find, studying mushrooms and collecting spore prints can be a lot of fun. Remember, though: NEVER eat a mushroom that you find outdoors. Eating just a tiny piece of a poisonous kind can make you seriously ill, or even kill you. Only experts can tell the difference between a dangerous mushroom and one that's okay to eat!

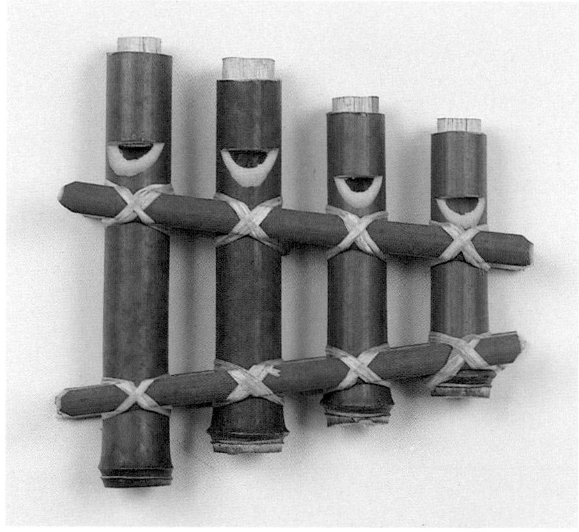

Pan Pipes

What You'll Need

- A length of bamboo*
- A small saw or hacksaw
- A piece of wooden stick or dowel
- A sharp penknife
- Glue
- String or twine

*If bamboo does not grow in your area, you can buy a cheap bamboo fishing pole at a sporting goods store.

What to Do

1. Saw off a length of bamboo about 6 or 8 inches long. It must have one end open and one end closed by a joint.

2. With the penknife, cut a sharp notch 1 inch from the open end of the bamboo. The notch must be cut through to the hollow part of the bamboo and must go about 1/3 of the way through the whole piece of bamboo.

3. Whittle out a 1-1/2 inch long wooden plug to go into the open end of the bamboo. It must fit snugly, but not split the bamboo. The plug must have a flat area carved on the top.

4. Put some glue on the plug and push it into the bamboo until it just gets to the edge of the notch. Be sure the flat area is on top of the plug.

5. Blow into the whistle and move the plug in and out until you get the best sound.

6. Make several whistles of different lengths and get each one adjusted to make a clear whistle sound.

7. Split a piece of bamboo into 4 strips and tie the strips to the whistles, one at a time, as shown in the photo.

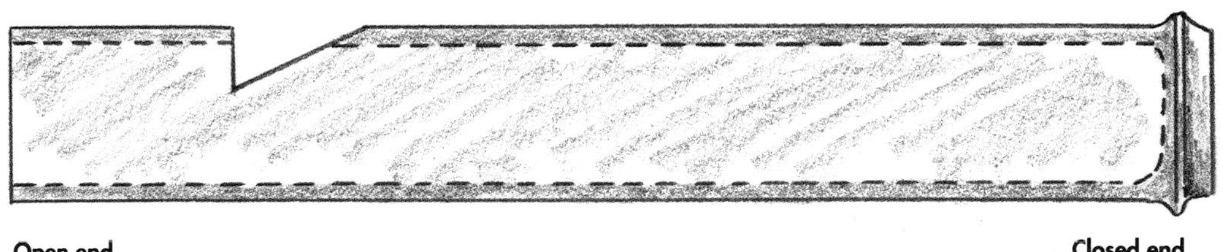

Herb Dolls

What You'll Need

- Fresh herbs
- A rubber band
- A piece of ribbon
- A doll's straw hat
- A hat pin

What to Do

1. Form a bunch of fresh herbs, and wrap a rubber band around their stem ends.
2. Tie a ribbon around the doll's "neck."
3. Attach a hat with a hat pin.
4. Hang the doll on the wall, or lean it wherever she's happy.

HERBS

If you asked everyone in your neighborhood to name one herb, chances are that most people would name a cooking herb, such as oregano. Most people don't know that an herb is any plant that has been used for cooking, as a medicine, or for its good smell. So the rose, which has been used for centuries to make teas and creams, is really an herb!

Scientists have found records of herbs dating back to Egypt in 2000 BC, where herb mixtures were used to preserve the bodies of kings and queens buried in the pyramids—in other words, to make mummies. Herbs have been used as medicines for centuries. By medieval times, almost everyone had a large garden of cooking herbs. Rich people used the fragrant herbs to cover up the bad smells of rotten meat (refrigerators had not been invented yet!), while poorer people lived on soups they made from herbs and water.

As time passed, food and housing became easier to find, and now people had time to care about other things, such as smell. Since they did not have toilets, toothbrushes, soaps, or showers, they were always in search of fragrant herbs that would make themselves smell better. When Victorian ladies had friends over to visit, they would carry a small bouquet of sweet-smelling herbs in front of their mouths to cover up their not-so-sweet breath. Victorians also disliked the damp, musky smells that came from the mud walls of their homes, so each home had a room called a stillroom where herbs and spices were made into perfumes to fragrance their clothes, furniture, and walls.

Herbs are still popular today, and they are used for many of the same reasons they were throughout history. We use them for making medicines like the heart drug digitalis, for making sauces, soups, and vinegars, and for making fragrant items such as soaps and candles.

Bath Bags

If you wrap up some sweet-smelling plants in a loose-weaved fabric and tie it up with a long piece of twine, you can hang the bag from the faucet in your bathtub. Then, while the tub fills, the water will pour through the bag, and you will have scented bath water.

What You'll Need

- Pieces of muslin about 8 or 10 inches square
- Dried herbs and flowers
- Yarn or twine

What to Do

1. Place a handful of dried herbs in the center of each square.
2. Bring the four corners together, and tie the bag up with yarn.

Plant Perfumes

What You'll Need

- Grain alcohol*
- Good-smelling flowers or leaves**
- Small glass bottles with tight-fitting caps
- For tags (optional): A pressed leaf or flower from the plant you used to make the perfume, paper, clear self-adhesive paper

*Don't use rubbing alcohol; it has too strong an odor. An adult will have to buy grain alcohol for you. (One well-known brand is Everclear.)
**Examples of good-smelling plants are dried rose petals, lavender leaves or flowers, mint leaves, jasmine flowers, and gardenia petals.

What to Do

1. Chop or cut the plant material into tiny pieces.
2. Put the pieces in a small bottle, and add the grain alcohol. Be sure to fill the bottle completely, so there is very little air in it.

3. Let the perfume sit for two weeks. Then uncap it and strain the perfume to remove the pieces of plant.
4. Smell the perfume. If it smells like the plant, recap the bottle and let it age for another week. If it doesn't smell strong enough, chop up some more of the plant, and let the perfume sit another two weeks.
5. If you like, make a pretty label for your perfume with a pressed leaf or flower. Lay the pressed plant on a small square of paper, then sandwich it between two small squares of clear contact paper. Punch a hole in the corner, thread a small ribbon or string through the hole, and tie it to the bottle.

Pet Collars

Fleas seem to hate the herb pennyroyal, although humans and animals find it very sweet-smelling. A collar stuffed with dried pennyroyal will help keep fleas off your pets. You can make either the loose style, worn by the dog in the pictures, or the tube style, which is more suitable for a cat.

For the Loose Style:

What You'll Need

- A cotton bandanna or other cotton fabric
- A sewing machine
- Matching thread
- Dried pennyroyal

What to Do

1. Cut the bandanna into a triangle. Make sure one end is long enough to tie comfortably around your dog's neck.
2. Fold over the top edge by about 3 inches. Get an adult to help you sew along the edge, creating a hollow tube. Leave one end open.
3. Stuff dried pennyroyal into the opening.
4. Sew up the opening..

For the Tube Style:

What You'll Need

- ■ A cotton bandanna or other cotton fabric
- ■ A sewing machine
- ■ A piece of Velcro about 3 inches long
- ■ Dried pennyroyal

What to Do

1. Measure your pet's neck. Cut the fabric 3 inches wide and 1/2 inch longer than your pet's neck measurement.
2. Fold the material in half with its right sides together, so you have a long skinny tube. Now sew up the long side and one of the short ends. Turn the tube inside out; the right side of the fabric should now be on the outside.
3. Sew half the Velcro piece on one end. (A piece of Velcro divides into 2 parts.)
4. Using a funnel to make it easier, stuff dried pennyroyal into the tube. Stop stuffing when you've filled the tube up to about 3 inches from the open end.
5. Sew the other half of the Velcro on the other end of the collar. Make sure it's on the opposite side from the first piece, so you can make a circle of the collar and attach it to your pet.

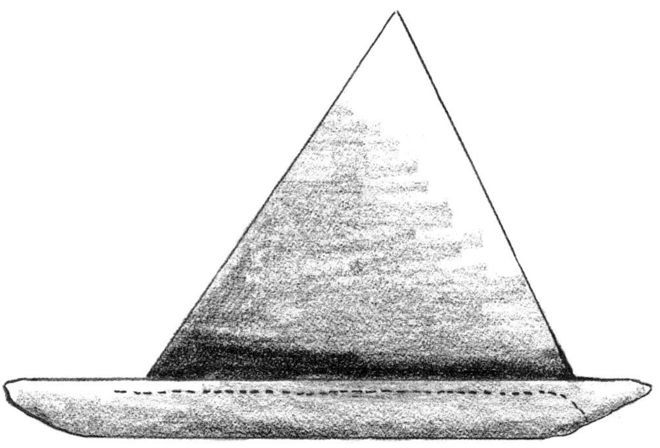

Loose style

Tube style

Ant House

What You'll Need

- Two glass jars with lids. One must be very narrow—like an olive jar, for example. The other must be slightly taller and wider, so the first jar can fit inside it.
- A spoon
- Ants
- Sand
- A small piece of wet sponge
- Honey
- An awl or nail, and a hammer
- 2 pieces dark* construction paper
- Scissors
- A stapler
- Tape
- A rubber band
- Light colored pencils or crayons

*The paper must be dark to keep the anthouse dark—the way the ants like it.

What to Do

1. Go outside and find some ants.
2. Put the lid on the smaller jar and place it inside the bigger one. Then carefully scoop some ants and the soil around them into the space between the two jars. Fill the jar about halfway with ants and soil.
3. Fill the rest of the bigger jar with sand. Use the stem end of the spoon to mix the sand and soil that are in the space. You do not have to mix it completely.
4. Put the piece of wet sponge and a small spoonful of honey into the jar, on top of the soil-and-sand mix. Then tightly put the lid on the bigger jar.
5. Use the awl or nail and the hammer to punch SMALL holes around the edges of the lid.
6. Cut a circle 8 inches in diameter out of dark construction paper. Make a cut from one edge to the center.
7. Curve the paper circle into a cone shape and staple it where the paper overlaps. Cut another piece of construction paper so that it's as tall as the flat side of the jar, and so that it reaches around the jar once with an inch overlap. Put a piece of clear tape down one short edge.
8. Wrap the paper around the jar. Tape the overlap. (The shiny surface of the edge you've already taped will make it possible for you to untape and retape the paper, so that you can check on your ants from time to time.)
9. Place the rubber band around the edge of the jar lid to help hold the roof of the house on.
10. Decorate the roof and sides of the house with colored pencils or crayons.
11. Set the roof on the house. Check on your ants in a day or so, and watch them tunnel and dig.

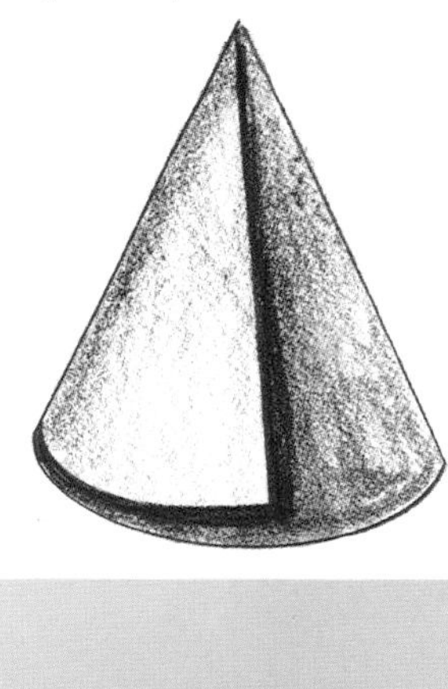

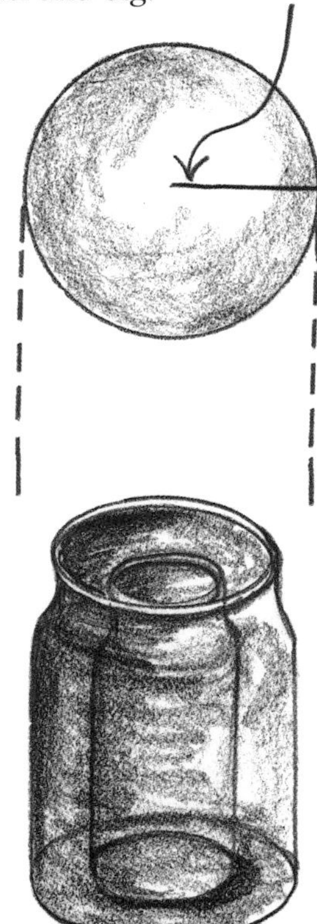

Pooter

A pooter is a device that helps you collect small insects without harming them. You'll suck them right into the jar.

What You'll Need

- A jar
- A rubber stopper that fits the jar tightly*
- 2 feet of flexible plastic tubing, about 1/4 inch inside diameter*
- Scissors
- A 1-inch square of gauze, cheesecloth, or screening
- A small rubber band
- A power drill with a large drill bit (1/4-inch works best)

*Look for the stopper and the plastic tubing in a store that sells wine-making supplies or in a hardware store.

What to Do

1. Get an adult to help you with the first step. With the power drill, drill two holes in the rubber stopper. (If your drill bit is narrower than your plastic tubing, tilt the drill from side to side to widen the hole as you drill.)

2. Cut the plastic tubing in half with scissors. Push each piece through one of the holes in the stopper. If you have trouble forcing the tubing through the holes, put a little dish detergent on the outside of the tubing to lubricate it.

3. Use the rubber band to fasten the gauze square over the end of one piece of tubing. Make sure you put it on an end that will be inside the jar.

4. Put the stopper in the mouth of the jar.

How to Use It

Go outside and look for a small insect. (It must be small enough to fit through the tubing!) Quietly walk up to the insect and place the end of the tube that does NOT have gauze as close as possible to the insect. Put the other tube—the tube with the gauze on it—in your mouth and suck on the other end of it. The insect will be vacuumed into the pooter by the suction. The gauze keeps the insect from being sucked into your mouth.

You can use a magnifying glass to study the insect. When you're finished studying it, unstop the pooter and release the insect into its environment.

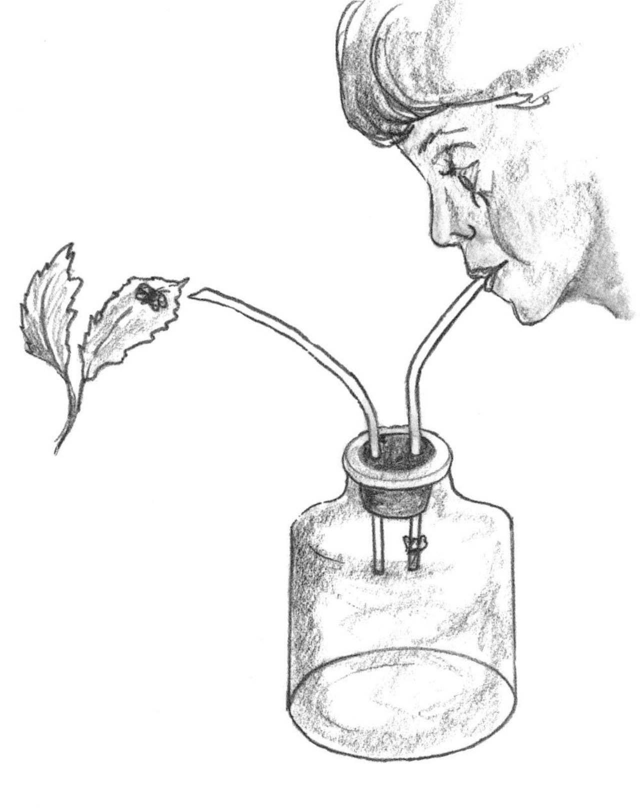

Bug Box

This handy box will hold all the creepy crawlies you catch this summer, as well as any food you need to give them. The screen admits all the air your new "pets" need, and you can watch them go about their business.

What You'll Need

- A board 3/4" by 3-1/2" by 24"
- A piece of 1/4" plywood
- A piece of screening 7-1/2" by 14-1/2"
- A piece of fiber splint 1/2" x 48"*
- A #6 x 3/4" wood screw
- 3/4" finishing nails
- 2 screw eyes
- A saw
- Wood glue
- A coat hanger
- Shears or heavy scissors for cutting screen
- A staple gun

*Fiber splint is used for weaving chair bottoms and is available in many craft stores. Reed for weaving baskets would work fine—or anything else flexible and smooth enough to cover the raw ends of the screening.

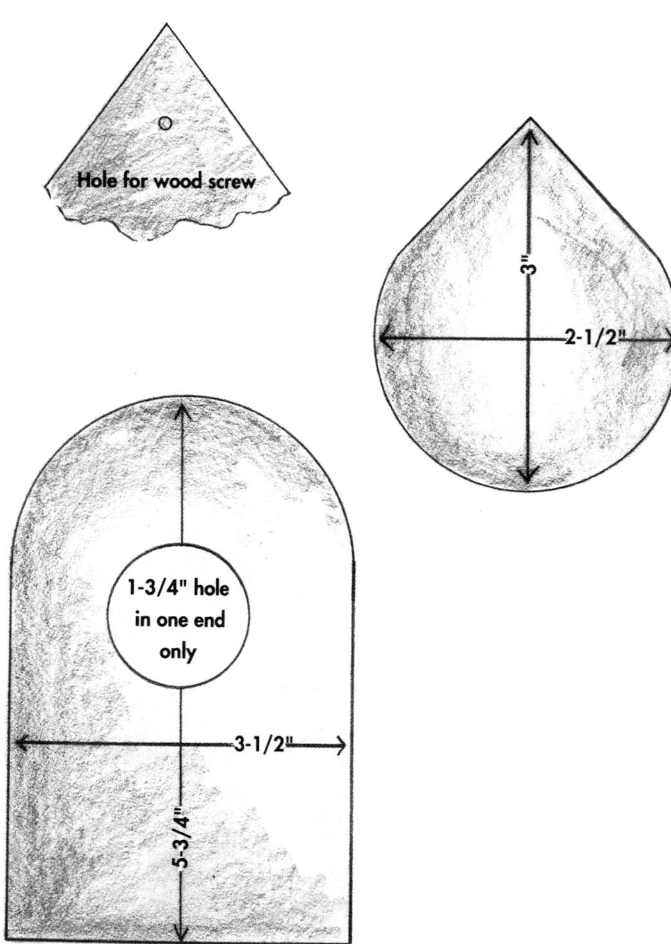

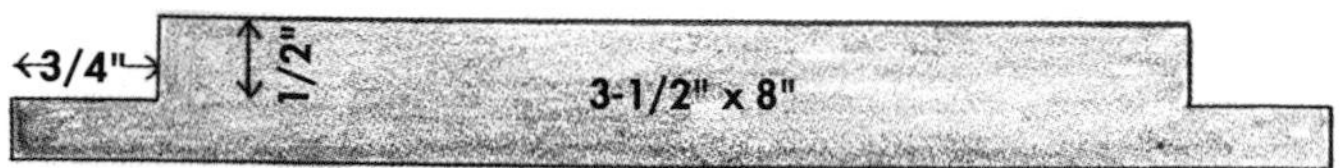

What to Do

1. Cut out all the wood pieces to the sizes shown on the drawing.
2. Cut or drill a 1-3/4" hole in one end piece.
3. Screw the door to this piece, using the wood screw. (Drill a hole for the screw first.)
4. Spread wood glue in the cut-out sections of the bottom, and stand the end pieces on top of the cut-out areas. Nail the ends to the bottom with the finishing nails. Let the frame dry.
5. Stretch the screening over the frame and staple it on. Cut off any excess screen.
6. Staple the fiber splint over the edges of the screen, as shown in the picture.
7. Using a nail, start holes at the top of each end, and screw in the screw eyes.
8. Cut and fold a wire coat hanger to make a handle, insert the ends through the screw eyes, and bend the ends so the handle will hold.

Sand Candles

If you're near a beach, it's fun to make your candles right on the beach by digging holes in the sand. If you aren't near the seashore, you can still make the candles look just as good.

What You'll Need

- A beach; or a plastic dishpan; or a heavy cardboard box lined with a plastic garbage bag
- Sand to fill the container*
- A spray bottle filled with water
- Seashells
- Paraffin or beeswax**
  1 pound will make 3 or 4 small candles or 1 large one.
- Old crayons
- A tin can
- A pan
- A hot pad or oven mit
- Candle wicking**
- A big paper clip
- A soft paint brush

*Sand can be found in discount marts and lumberyards.

**Paraffin can be found in grocery stores and discount marts, alongside the canning supplies. Beeswax and candle wicking are sold in craft stores.

What to Do

1. Fill the dishpan or box with damp sand, and pat it smooth and level.
2. Dig a hole the size and shape you want your candle to be. Spray the sand with water if it crumbles.
3. Press seashells into the sides of the hole, with the shells' right sides facing the sand.
4. Ask an adult to help you melt the paraffin or wax. Place the paraffin or wax in the tin can, and add a

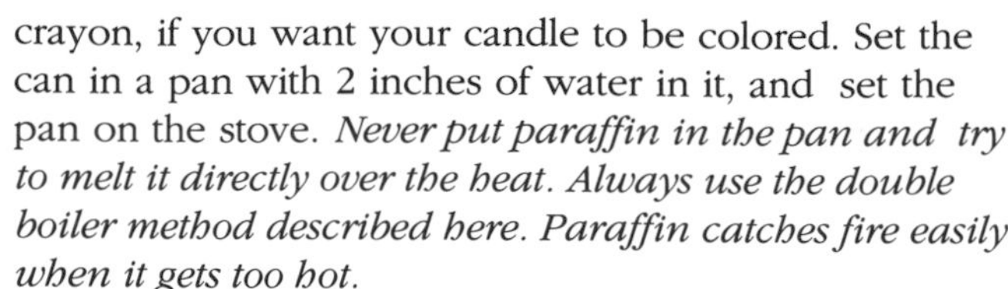

crayon, if you want your candle to be colored. Set the can in a pan with 2 inches of water in it, and set the pan on the stove. *Never put paraffin in the pan and try to melt it directly over the heat. Always use the double boiler method described here. Paraffin catches fire easily when it gets too hot.*

5. Dip a piece of wicking 4 inches longer than your candle in melted wax. Let it cool for 5 minutes, until it's stiff.

6. Place the dried wick in the middle of the sand hole. If the bottom of the hole will be the top of the candle, stick the wick an inch or so into the bottom of the hole. Hold onto the wick while you go onto the next step.

7. Using a hot pad or oven mitt, carefully pour the melted wax into the hole, filling it to the top.

8. As the wax cools, an air pocket may form beneath the surface. Use a straightened-out paper clip to poke a hole in the wax skin. The skin may then collapse, and you will need to add more wax. You may need to repeat this step several times.

9. Let the candle cool for a couple of hours, or longer if it's a big one. Don't move the pan of sand.

10. When the candle is hard, gently dig the sand away from the edge with your finger. Soon you'll be able to grasp the candle and wiggle it like a loose tooth. Wiggle it out of the sand.

11. Stand the candle on the sand and gently brush the loose sand off, using a soft paint brush. Damp sand will stick to the candle, but it will dry quickly and you'll be able to brush it off. The finished candle will look sandy, and your seashells will peek through like shells on the beach at low tide.

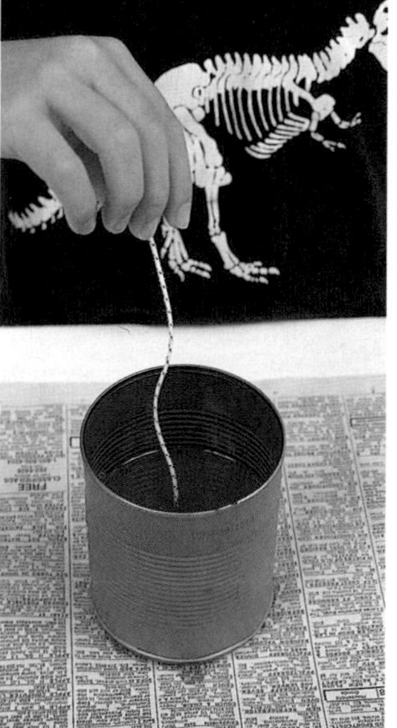

THE AMAZING OCEAN

The ocean covers more than 70% of the Earth, or about 140 million square miles. It contains 97% of all the water in the world.

Although the ocean is actually one huge body of water, geographers divide it into four major oceans: the Pacific, Atlantic, Indian, and Arctic. The largest is the Pacific, which stretches across 64 million square miles, or about one-third of the planet. You could fit all the world's continents (North and South America, Europe, Asia, Africa, Australia and Antarctica) into the Pacific, and there'd still be over 7,000 square miles of sea left.

The deepest place in the ocean is in the Mariana Trench, in the western Pacific. The water there is over 6-1/2 miles (about 36,000 feet) deep. If you put the world's tallest mountain, Mt. Everest, into the Mariana Trench, the mountain's peak would be more than a mile beneath the water's surface!

The land under the sea has plains, hills, mountains, and valleys much like the land we live on. In some places, there are huge gorges and canyons at least as big as America's Grand Canyon. The highest underwater mountain, in the Pacific Ocean between New Zealand and the island of Samoa, is 28,500 feet tall. It's actually the second biggest mountain in the world.

Fish Print

What You'll Need

- A whole fish, cleaned but with the head on*
- Old newspapers
- Tempera paint
- A large, soft paint brush, about 1 inch wide
- Paper for the print**

*One way to get a whole fish is to catch your own. If you don't fish, the next easiest is a fish market or the meat department in the grocery store. If you don't see any whole fish on display, ask the person behind the counter to get a whole fish for you. Tell him or her that you want the fish cleaned but not scaled and that you want the head left on. Fish that are rather flat work best.
**The best kind of paper to use is Japanese block printing paper, which you can get in an art supply store. You can also use tissue paper or white shelf paper or soft drawing paper. The paper should be strong enough to stand up under wet paint. Shiny paper won't hold paint well.

What to Do

1. Lay the fish on a piece of old newspaper, and paint the entire fish with tempera paint.
2. Carefully lift the fish, trying not to touch the painted surfaces, and place it, painted side up, on a clean piece of newspaper.
3. Lay the piece of print paper over the fish, being careful not to move the paper once it touches the fish.

4. Gently rub the paper where it lies over the fish. Be sure not to move the paper.
5. Carefully peel the paper back from the fish and lay it flat to dry.
6. Use the fish print to make a simple banner, to decorate a carp kite (see page 24), to wrap a present, or to cover a book.

Banner

What You'll Need

- A fish print
- Rubber cement
- Scissors
- 2 pieces of bamboo, each as long as the paper is wide. (If you don't have any of your own to cut, you can buy slender bamboo in a garden supply store where sticks are sold as tomato stakes.)
- Yarn

What to Do

1. Turn the print right side down, and fold down 1 inch along both the top and bottom edges of the paper.
2. Brush a thin line of rubber cement along the very edge of each fold, and press the fold to the paper. Remember, you're creating a "tunnel" for the bamboo stick, so don't glue down the whole flap.
3. Cut tabs about an inch apart all along the two edges
4. Thread the bamboo poles through the tabs.
5. Cut a long piece of yarn and tie its ends to the ends of the top piece of bamboo, so that you can hang the banner.

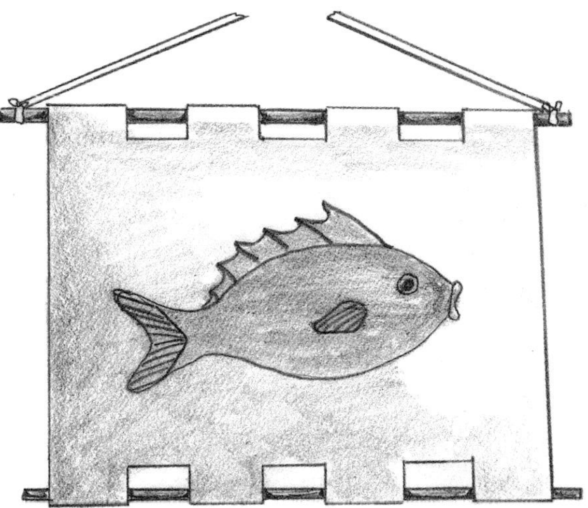

Sand Painting

What You'll Need

- Powdered tempera paints*
- Sand—the whiter and finer, the better
- Small containers to mix colored sand in
- A spoon for each color
- A clean, dry glass jar or bottle
- Improvised tools for moving sand around, such as an opened-out paperclip, small, flat plastic sticks, etc.

*Look for them at a school supply store or craft store. If you can find only liquid tempera paints, you can use them too. But after you color the sand, you'll have to let it dry for a few days before you paint with it.

What to Do

1. Put about 1 cup of sand in each container. Add some paint, and stir until the color is even. Try mixing different colors together until you get a color you like.
2. Spoon the first layer of colored sand into the jar.

WHAT IS SAND?

If you take a rock and pound it with a hammer hard enough and long enough, you'll make sand. Nature does the same thing, but instead of a hammer it uses water, wind, and weather to crush rocks into tiny pieces.

All over the world, from the highest mountains to the ocean shores, nature is battering away at rocks to create the gritty material we call sand. Rain washes it into the soil and into streams and rivers, where it rolls along downstream. Eventually, much of the sand is washed out to sea.

Meanwhile, ocean waves constantly churn up rocks in the water and smash them together with other rocks, rock fragments, and sand. Gradually big pieces become small pieces, small pieces become tiny fragments, coarse sand becomes fine sand. Storms, tides, waves, and currents move the sand around. Some of it ends up on shore to make beaches and dunes. Some is buried at the bottom of the sea in huge piles.

There are many kinds of rocks, so there are many kinds of sand. Quartz, which is usually white or clear, is the most common mineral in sand. It comes from granite, a type of rock found almost everywhere in the world. Some beaches in Hawaii and other Pacific islands are made of black sand, which is actually grains of worn-down hardened lava, from volcanoes. Most beach sand also contains tiny bits of seashells and coral. Some beaches, such as Florida's famous white sand beaches, are made almost entirely of shell sand!

Make it as deep as you want, and smooth the top.

3. Carefully add the second color of sand right on top of the first. When it's as deep as you want and smooth on top, slide one of your flat tools down the side of the jar to move the sand into shapes.

This takes some practice, but soon you'll be able to push shapes into the bottom layer and then push the second layer to fill in the spaces that were left.

4. Smooth the second layer, adding more sand if you need to.

5. Add the other layers the same way. For variety, you can make a small section of a layer a different color from the rest. You can also push a shape into a layer and fill just that shape with a small amount of a different color.

How to Use It

Your sand painting makes a good candle holder. Or set a small potted plant on top. Or make a colorful terrarium in a large container, such as a gallon jar. Do the sand painting on the bottom 2 or 3 inches. Then top the sand painting with 4 inches of soil, add small plants, spray them with water, and cover the jar.

Beach Basket

What You'll Need

- Long grasses and sedges gathered from wetlands and dunes near the beach
- Vines, such as honeysuckle and grape
- Hand snippers or pruners
- A garbage bag
- An empty 1-gallon plastic milk jug with the top cut off

What to Do

1. Check with an adult before you go out to gather materials. Some grasses, such as sea oats, are endangered species and should never be picked. Be sure the grasses you want to gather are okay to pick. Take along a garbage bag to carry your grasses in and a pair of garden snippers or pruners for cutting.

Look at the back of the beach along the dunes or at a salt marsh near the beach for the longest grasses and sedges you can find. (Grasses have hollow, round stems. Sedges have solid, triangular-shaped stems.)

It's best to gather vines in fall or winter because they don't have so much juice in them then, and they are tougher and stronger. If you have to gather in spring or summer, pick the older part of the vine rather than the tender, new growth. The best vines for this basket are about as big around as a pencil—no bigger. Remove all leaves as you cut vines, but leave the curly tendrils on grapevines if you like the way they look.

2. You can store basketry materials for as long as you want. Be sure to keep them out of the sun in a cool, dry place. It's better NOT to store them in plastic bags, as they will mildew. Hang them up or stand them loosely in a trash can or small garbage can until you're ready to use them.

When you are ready to work, soak the materials for at least an hour in a tub full of water. If the materials are newly picked, you may not need to soak them at all. To see if they need soaking or if they have soaked long enough, wind an end of a vine or piece of grass around your finger. It should go around your finger

without breaking. Some vines have light bark on them that might crack when you wind the vine around your finger. If the inside of the vine doesn't break, you can go ahead and use the material.

3. To make the basket, first cut 8 *stakes* out of vines. Cut the stakes about 3 feet long, all the same length.

4. Lay 4 of the stakes side by side crossways on top of the other 4 stakes, as in Figure 1.

5. Select a long piece of grass or sedge or a slender vine to be the first *weaver.* Holding the tail of the weaver in place, wrap the weaver over 4 of the stakes that are ON TOP OF the cross, under the next 4 stakes, over the next 4, and under the last 4. Continue going over 4/under 4 for 3 more rounds. The bottom of your basket should now look like Figure 2.

6. At the end of the 4th round, bend the weaver around the 4 stakes it has just gone over, and go UNDER those 4 stakes, headed in the opposite direction (look at Figure 3). Go 4 rounds of over 4/under 4, just as you did before. The bottom of the basket should now look like Figure 4.

7. You will now begin BREAKING DOWN the groups of

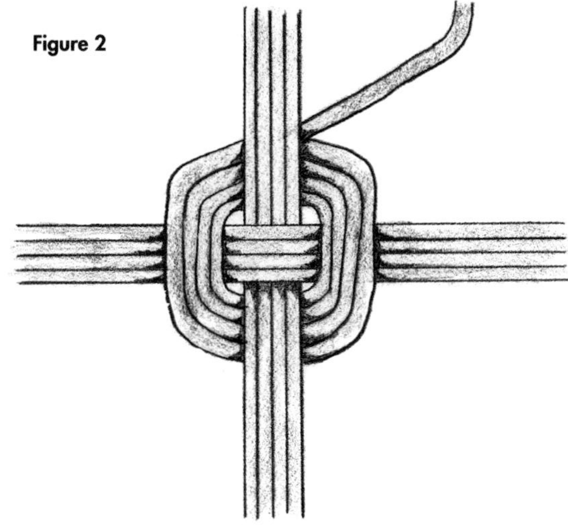

Figure 2

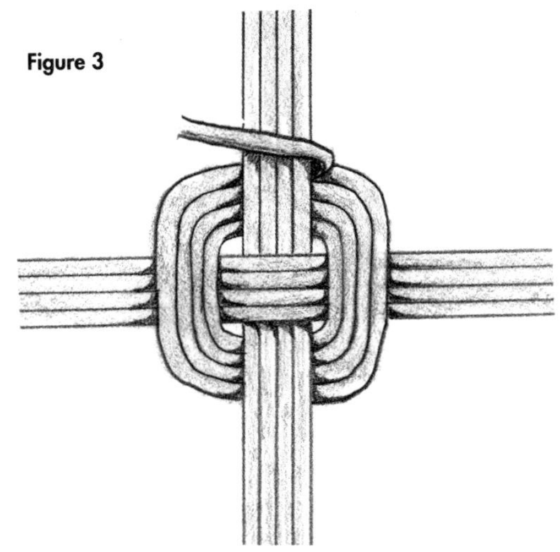

Figure 3

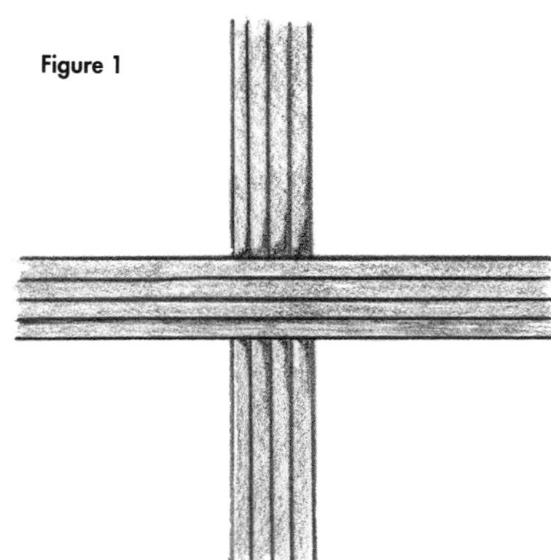

Figure 1

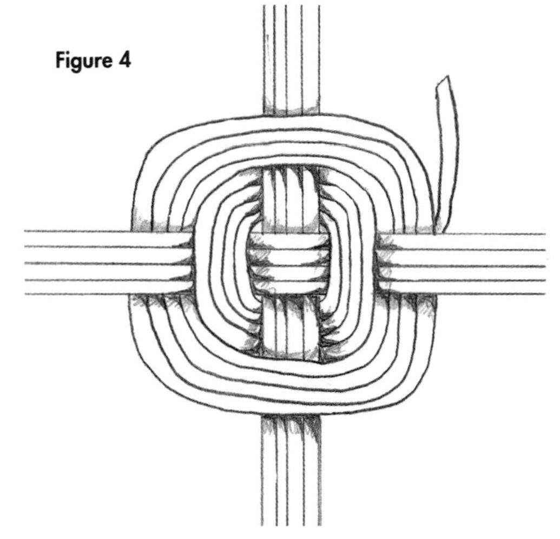

Figure 4

4 into groups of 2. Continue going over and under in the same direction, but this round go over 2/under 2. Pull the groups of 4 stakes apart as you weave, as in Figure 5.

8. When you get back to pair #1, you will notice something: if you went OVER pair #2 as you would if you kept going over 2/under 2, you would find that you would be placing your weaver exactly as it was on the last round, giving you two "overs" on the same pair of stakes. To avoid this problem, when you get back to #1, go UNDER it, even though you just went under #8. Then continue as usual, going OVER the next 2, under the next 2, etc. Each time you get back to #1 you will have to make this same adjustment and go the opposite way that you would expect to go. Just remember that your stakes, as well as your weavers, should look like Figure 6 (over-under-over-under).

9. Weave a few rounds with pairs of stakes, and then break down to single stakes. That is, go over 1/under 1.

10. As you weave, you'll need to add new weavers every round or so. To do that, simply hold the first few inches of the new weaver with the last few inches of the old weaver and use them together. As the old

Figure 5

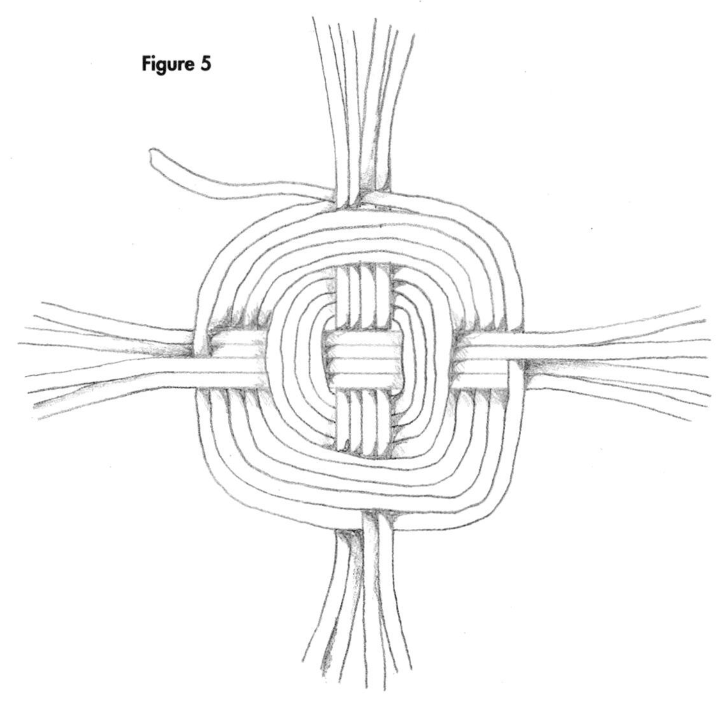

Figure 6

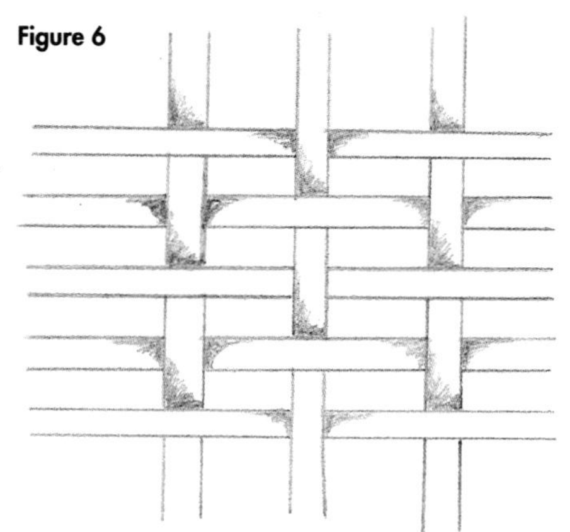

Figure 7

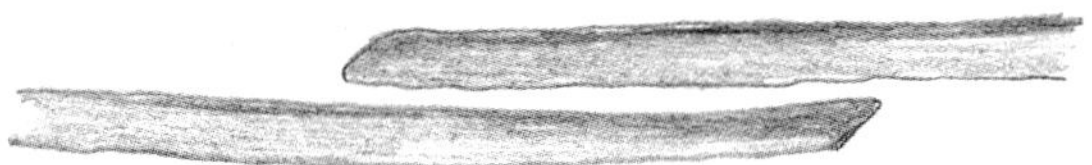

Figure 8

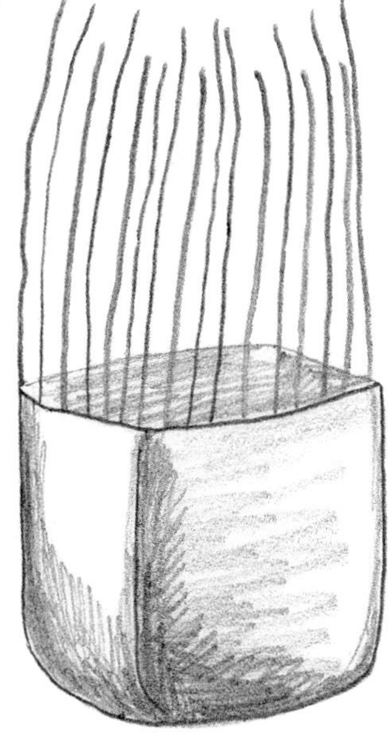

weaver ends, the new one will already be attached and can take over. See Figure 7.

11. After you have made the bottom of the basket the size you want it to be, you will need to curve the walls upward and inward. An easy way to do this is to gather all the stakes in the center, and then push the bottom down into the empty milk carton, as in Figure 8.

Let the basket sit for an hour or so. When you take it out, the stakes will be curved up into the shape of the walls of the basket.

12. Continue weaving until you are about 4 inches from the ends of the stakes (Figure 9). You can stop sooner if you want a smaller basket, but don't let the ends of the stakes get any shorter than about 4 inches or it will be very difficult to make a border on the basket.

13. To make a border, soak the stake ends until they are flexible. Then bend each stake over in front of the stake just after itself. As you go around the rim bending the stakes, a simple braid will form and the stakes will hold each other down and in place. Poke the end of the last stake under the first folded-over stake, as in Figure 10.

14. Trim any long ends with garden pruners.

Figure 10

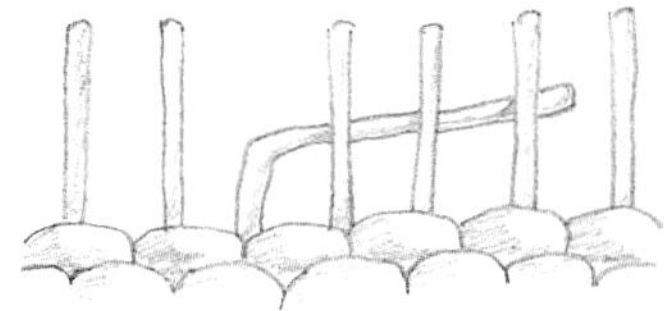

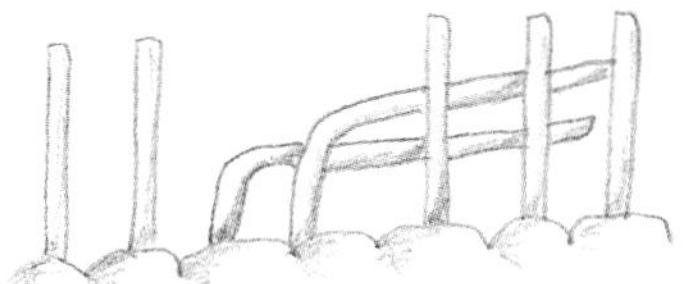

Figure 9

AUTUMN

Leaf Stained Glass

What You'll Need

- Waxed paper
- Pressed leaves*
- Scissors
- An iron
- Old newspapers.

*See page 41 for directions for pressing flowers and leaves.

What to Do

1. Tear off two pieces of waxed paper a little larger than you want your finished stained glass to be.
2. Lay one piece of waxed paper on top of several sections of old newspaper.
3. Arrange the leaves on the waxed paper.
4. Put the second piece of waxed paper on top of the leaves.
5. With the iron set on "low," gently press the waxed paper sandwich. You will see the pieces of paper joining together. Keep moving the iron in circles until the whole top piece of paper is fused to the leaves and to the bottom paper.
6. Trim the edges of the waxed paper to make them straight.
7. Hang your stained glass in a window using cellophane tape

WHY DO LEAVES TURN COLORS IN AUTUMN?

Nature really shows off in autumn, when the leaves on trees and shrubs in most parts of the top half of the world burst into colors. It's almost as though someone painted them. But actually, the secret of nature's artistry is inside the leaves. That's where, during the spring and summer, a substance called chlorophyll (pronounced klor-o-fill) uses energy from the sun to help make food for the plant. Chlorophyll is also what makes leaves green.

But there are other colors in leaves, too. It's just that, during the growing season, there's so much bold green chlorophyll you can't see the others. In the fall, though, the chlorophyll slowly fades, and the "shy" colors pop out, as if to say, "See? We're here, too!" The hidden colors are yellows, oranges, reds, browns, and even purple.

Some plants have mostly just one color in them. Poplar leaves, for instance, are strictly bright yellow, and sugar maple leaves are fiery red. Other leaves are a mixture of colors. Oak leaves, for example, have yellow, orange, and brown in them. Depending on how much of each color is mixed in, oak leaves can be anything from bright gold to dull bronze.

Some autumns are more colorful than others. Weather is the reason why. Usually, cool temperatures and lots of sunshine make an especially bright and beautiful fall leaf show. But if there was little rain during the summer, there will be more brown or dull-colored leaves and fewer bright red ones.

Leaf Collection Box

If you like to gather leaves, it's fun to save your collection. Just press the leaves, glue each one to an index card, and cover it with clear self-adhesive shelf paper. Then file it in a box you've decorated. For example, the leaves in the picture are all from scented geraniums, so they're filed under "G."

What You'll Need

- A wooden file box, the kind that holds index cards*
- Extra-fine sandpaper or steel wool
- Petroleum jelly
- A household sponge, cut into pieces about 2 inches by 1 inch
- Green acrylic paint**
- A paper plate
- A red paint pen
- A spray can of clear acrylic sealer**

*Wooden file boxes are sold in craft stores and office supply stores.
**Acrylic paints and acrylic sealer are sold in craft stores and art supply stores.

What to Do

1. With the sandpaper or steel wool, lightly sand the sides of the box you're going to paint on.
2. It's best to work on one side of the box at a time. Put a dab of petroleum jelly in the center of each leaf and then position it on the box, jelly side down, smoothing it out. The jelly will hold the leaf in place temporarily.
3. When you've put all the leaves where you want them on one side of the box, put a little green paint on a paper plate. Dampen a piece of sponge, and dip it into the paint. Dab paint over and around the leaves on the box. Be careful not to move the leaves.
4. When the paint has dried, remove the leaves and wipe off any jelly that's left with a tissue.
5. Then do the other sides of the box the same way.
6. Use the red paint pen to add red dots where the box looks a little blank. The dots will look like little red berries.
7. When the paint is very dry, spray the painted sides with clear acrylic sealer, to protect it.

WHY DO TREES DROP THEIR LEAVES?

Animals get ready for the winter by adding more fat and growing thicker fur to keep warm. Trees get ready by dropping their leaves to keep from dying of thirst.

Leaves use up huge amounts of water. That's no problem most of the year, but in the winter, when the ground is frozen, a tree can't draw water in through its roots. It has to survive mostly on just the water stored in its trunk and branches. A leafy tree would quickly use up all the water and die. But a leafless tree can live on stored water for months.

So, as the weather gets colder and the leaves turn colors, a thin, soft layer forms between each leaf's stem and the twig or branch. All it takes to break the layer is a gust of wind, and the leaf comes tumbling down.

That's not the end of the story, though. On the ground beneath the tree, all the leaves gradually soften and fall apart. Before long they become part of the soil. Their nutrients are drawn up through the roots, into the tree itself, and eventually up to the leaves again.

In a way, then, leaves never really die. They just recycle themselves.

NEEDLE KNOWLEDGE

Most evergreens have leaves that look like needles. Many people think that evergreen trees never lose their leaves, but they do. Most types actually do shed their needles, but not all at once the way oaks and maples do. Instead, they drop their leaves gradually, continually replacing the ones that are lost with new needles.

What really sets evergreen leaves apart is their ability to survive winter. Their tough, thick skin and waxy coating protect them from freezing or drying out during cold, windy weather.

If you look closely at an evergreen's leaves, you can tell what kind of tree it is.

■ *If the needles are pointed and are growing in bunches,* with each group stuck together at the bottom by a little papery strip, you're looking at a pine tree. Only pine trees grow needles in clusters.

■ *If the needles are stiff and sharp and are growing all around the branch,* it's a spruce tree. Spruce needles actually have four sides.

■ *If the needles are flat and short with rounded ends and are growing opposite each other on the branch,* it's either a fir tree or a hemlock tree. But now look at the tree's top. If it's straight and pointed like a big spear, you've found a fir tree. If the top is sort of droopy-looking, the tree is a hemlock.

■ *If the "needles" are actually branches or twigs covered by tiny flat, green triangular leaves,* the tree is probably a cedar or cypress.

Evergreen Garland

What You'll Need

- Fresh evergreen branches. (You can use all one kind or mix in several different kinds.)
- Dried flowers, if you like
- Flexible wire
- Heavy cord or wire, for the spine*
- Scissors

*Jute cord, the kind used for macrame craft projects, works well. So does a heavy-gauge wire, available in hardware stores.

What to Do

1. Cut the evergreens into small branches, about 6 to 8 inches long. If you're using dried flowers to add color, cut their stems about the same length or shorter.
2. Take a handful of branches and wire them together by their stems, using the flexible wire.
3. Make a whole series of these bunches, using your greenery and flowers any way you want. You can make a bunch of all one thing—all greens, all flowers—or combine different things in each bunch.
4. Cut the heavy cord or wire—the spine of the garland—as long as you want the garland to be.
5. Using the flexible wire, attach one of the bunches you've made to the spine. Just wrap the wire around the stems and the spine. Start at one end of the spine.
6. Then wire a second bunch onto the spine. Point the bunches in the same direction, and make sure the greenery from the second bunch overlaps the stems of the first.
7. Keep wiring on bunches of greenery and flowers until you've covered the spine. Then tie a knot in each end of the cord.
8. If you want, you can attach other decorations. Just glue these to it with tacky glue.

Paper with Inlaid Leaves

What You'll Need

- A blender
- Scraps of old paper torn into small pieces*
- Water
- A plain wooden picture frame, 8 x 10 inches or larger
- A piece of window screen material, 12 x 14 inches or larger
- A staple gun or some waterproof glue
- Pressed leaves or flower petals
- A large plastic dishpan or baby bathtub
- Some clean rags, at least 15 x 15 inches square
- Old newspapers
- A rolling pin
- Metal shears or scissors to cut the screen
- A bottle of chlorine bleach (optional)

*Soft, thick paper is best. You can also use lint from a dryer.

What to Do

1. Put the torn scraps of paper and water in the blender to soak.
2. Meanwhile, stretch the screen over the picture frame and staple it into place.
3. Blend the paper and water until it's smooth mush. If you're using dryer lint or any colored paper scraps and you want your paper to be white, add 1/4 cup of chlorine bleach to the blender.
4. Pour batches of mush into the tub, adding a little water if the mush is too thick, until you have around 5 inches of mushy water in the dishpan or baby bathtub.
5. Place the pressed leaves in a handy spot near the pan of mush.
6. Dip the frame under the mush; then, holding it level, shift it back and forth until a layer of mush settles evenly over the surface. This layer should be around 1/2 inch thick.
7. Without tilting the frame, lift frame and mush layer out of the dishpan. Hold the frame over the pan to let water drain out. If the mush clumps together or if there are holes, put the frame back under the mush layer and try again.
8. As soon as you have drained most of the water from the mush on the frame, press flattened leaves or flower petals into the layer of mush in a pleasing arrangement. They need not be completely covered, but must be at least partially covered or they won't stay on the paper

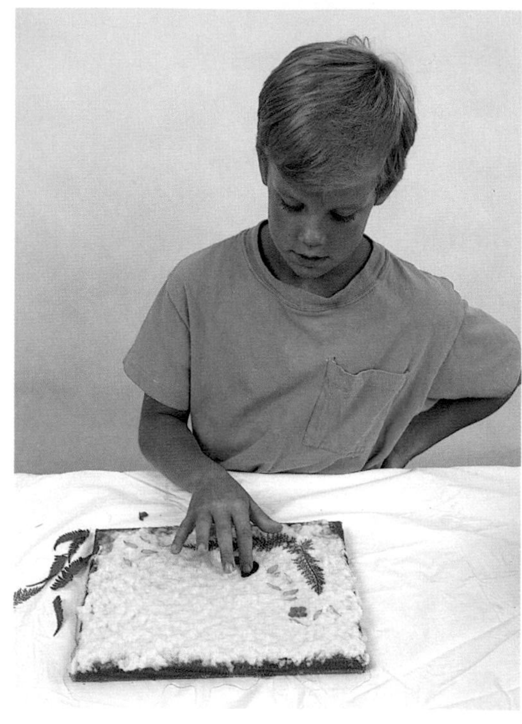

when it dries. You can gently push some mush over the leaves to help bury them.

9. Place a clean rag over the top of the drained mush layer. Press down gently, squeezing out more water.

10. Lay a few pieces of old newspaper down on a table. Carefully turn the frame, wet paper, and rag upside down onto the newspaper, and lift off the frame. Cover the wet paper with another rag. You now have a sandwich of two rags with a layer of wet paper in the middle.

11. Roll the sandwich with the rolling pin to press out even more water.

12. Carefully peel off the top rag. Turn the wet paper and bottom rag over onto either a smooth counter top or a piece of glass (you can use a window for this), paper side down, and then carefully peel off the remaining rag.

13. Let the paper dry overnight or longer.

14. If you want very smooth paper, spray the dry paper with spray laundry starch, put a clean smooth rag over the damp paper, and iron it with a slightly warm iron until the paper is dry. The starch will make the paper better for writing on, too.

15. You can use your inlaid paper to make cards, to wrap presents, for a cover for a handmade book, to write notes on, or in a window as a decorative window covering.

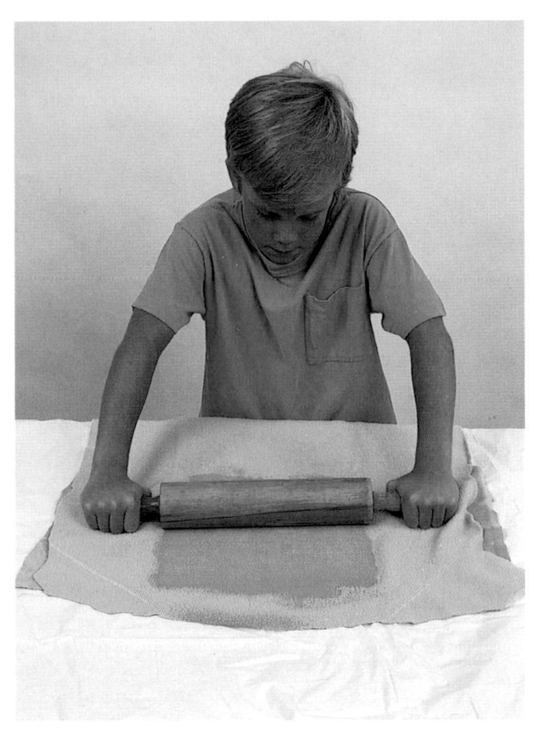

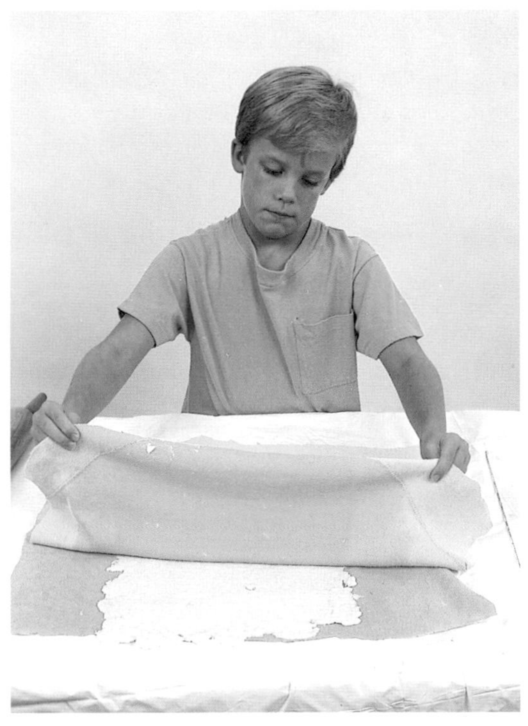

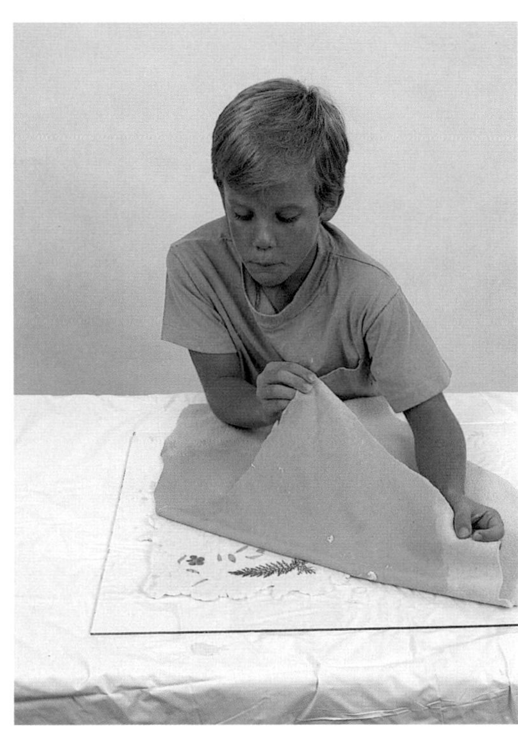

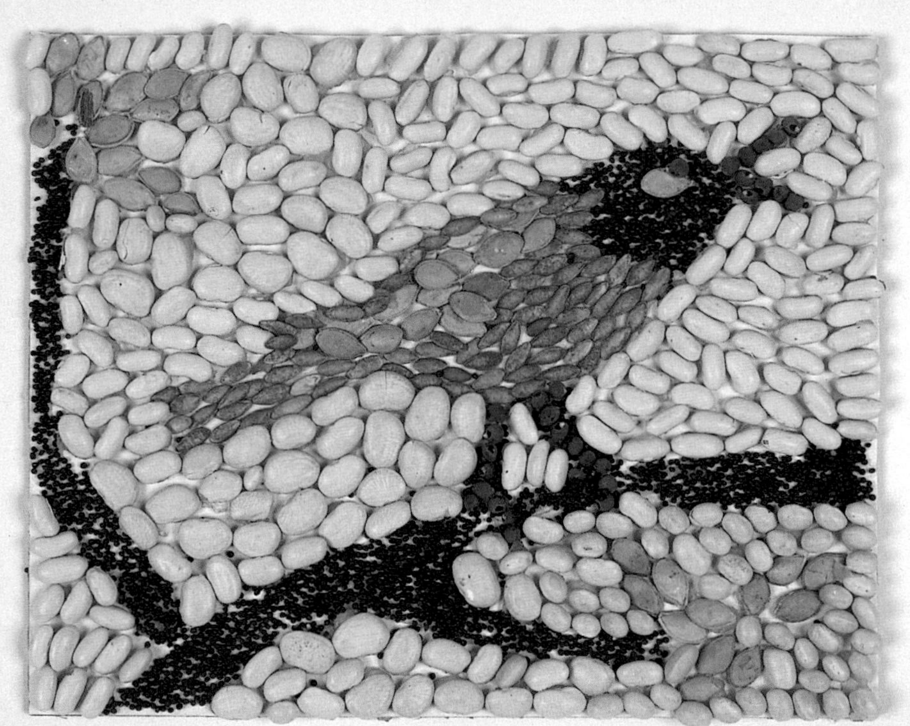

Seed Mosaic

What You'll Need

- A piece of heavy cardboard
- A pencil
- White glue
- A variety of seeds

What to Do

1. Sketch your design lightly on the cardboard. You can draw real things, like animals, or just sketch in shapes that please you.
2. Glue the seeds on the cardboard to fill in your design.
3. For very tiny seeds, use a paintbrush to paint glue on the cardboard, then sprinkle the seeds onto the glue. Use your fingers to push the seeds in place. After a few minutes, turn the cardboard over and lightly tap the back, so that the extra seeds can fall off.

TRAVELING SEEDS

Seeds are nature's way of spreading plants around. If a seed falls straight to the ground beneath the mother plant and starts to grow, it has to compete with the bigger plant for sunlight, food, and water. Seeds get a much better start in life if they travel to new ground.

Many seeds, like the puffy "parachute" seeds of the dandelion, ride the wind. A dandelion flower launches hundreds of tiny seed travelers, each with its own cluster of silky hairs to keep it in the air as long as possible. Poplar and willow trees have very light seeds with a little balloon of cottony fluff that catches the breeze and can sail for miles.

Maple, elm, and ash trees send out winged seeds that twirl and spin like helicopter blades. The seeds are quite heavy, but they grow high up among the branches, where winds are strong enough to blow the "whirlybirds" to new soil.

Pinecones and the cones from other evergreens are full of "flying" seeds. Young cones are green and their scales are closed tight. But gradually the cones become dry and brown, and the seeds inside ripen. The cones open up and the papery seeds flutter away in the breeze. Most cones on the ground have already let their seeds go. If you can find a ripe cone still on the tree, peel it apart and toss the seeds into the air to see how they fly.

The seeds in fruits and berries get to their new location in a different way: They ride inside the stomachs of the birds and animals that eat them. Most seeds can't be digested, so they come out with their own little pile of manure fertilizer to help them grow.

Other seeds ride on animals—and on people, too. If you've ever taken a

A jewelweed flower

walk in some weeds and found your pants and socks covered with stickers and prickly burrs, you know how. Burdock, tickseed, and lots of other wild plants have seed cases covered with little hooks or spines that cling to fur and clothing. That's how some plants got from the New World to Europe (and vice-versa)—the seeds hitched a ride on the clothes of early explorers!

Ground squirrels and blue jays are the world's best planters of oak tree seeds. Both like to bury acorns, one at a time in its own hole, to be eaten later. But they don't always come back to get the nuts. Wildlife biologists say that's why oak trees often outnumber others types in forests.

Some plants literally throw their seeds to new soil! Jewelweed plants are called "touch-me-nots" because, if you touch a seed pod, it bursts open with a pop and hurls a shower of seeds in every direction. Witch hazel pods explode with so much force they toss their brown, shiny seeds as far as 40 feet!

Another clever traveler is the seed from alder trees, which grow along streams and rivers. Each little seed, dropped from small cones on the alder's branches, has tiny pockets of air that keep it afloat as it cruises downstream to a muddy growing place.

Twig and Cone Wreath

What You'll Need

- A wire coat hanger
- Lots of twigs
- Flexible wire
- Shears or heavy scissors
- Cones
- Berries
- Tacky glue

What to Do

1. Untwist the handle of the coat hanger, bend the coat hanger into a circle, and retwist it closed.
2. Cut several pieces of wire about 6 inches long. Green floral wire, available in craft stores, is excellent, but any fine-gauge wire will work.
3. Take a handful of twigs and form them into a bunch. Wrap a piece of wire around the bunch at one end, and twist the ends of the wire together so the twigs stay together.
4. When you have several bunches made, start the wreath. Hold a bunch against the coat hanger circle, and wire it on with another piece of wire.
5. Wire on a second bunch of twigs, overlapping the wired ends of the first. Keep adding bunches of twigs until the coat hanger is covered.
6. With tacky glue, glue on small or medium-size cones wherever they look good. For extra color, glue on some bright berries.
7. Let the glue dry, then hang the wreath on a door, on a mantle, or on the wall.

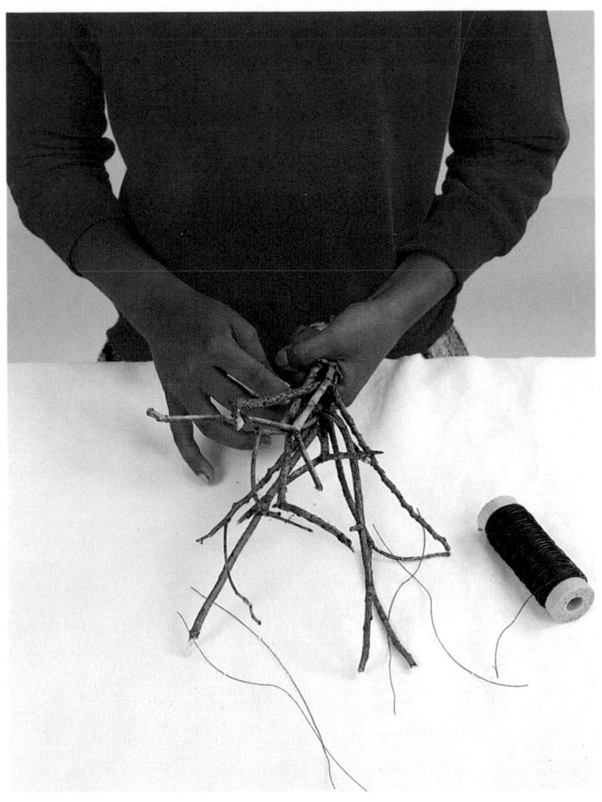

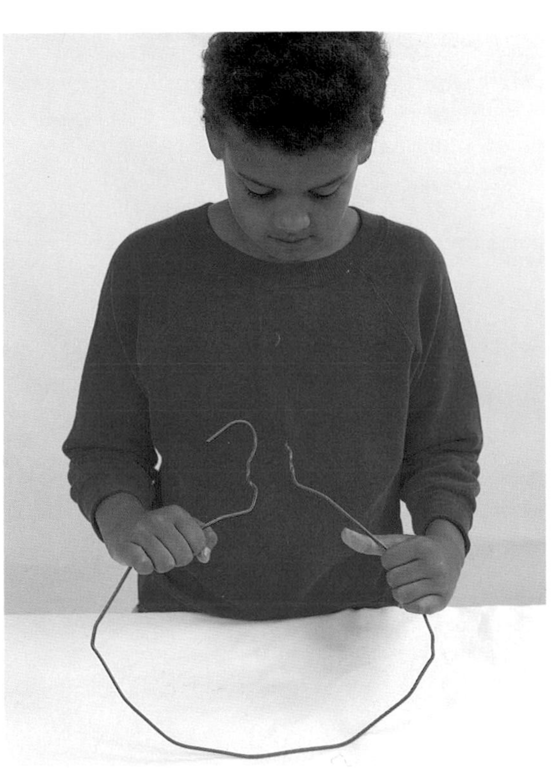

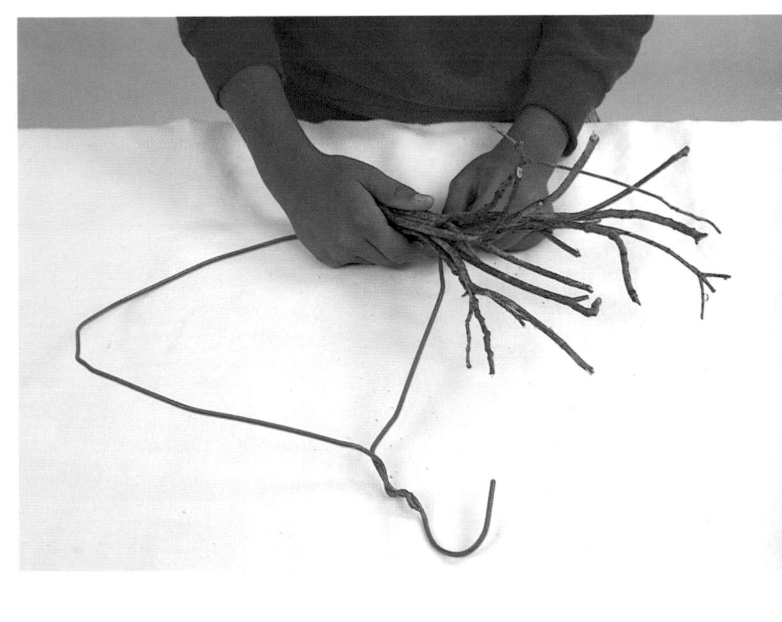

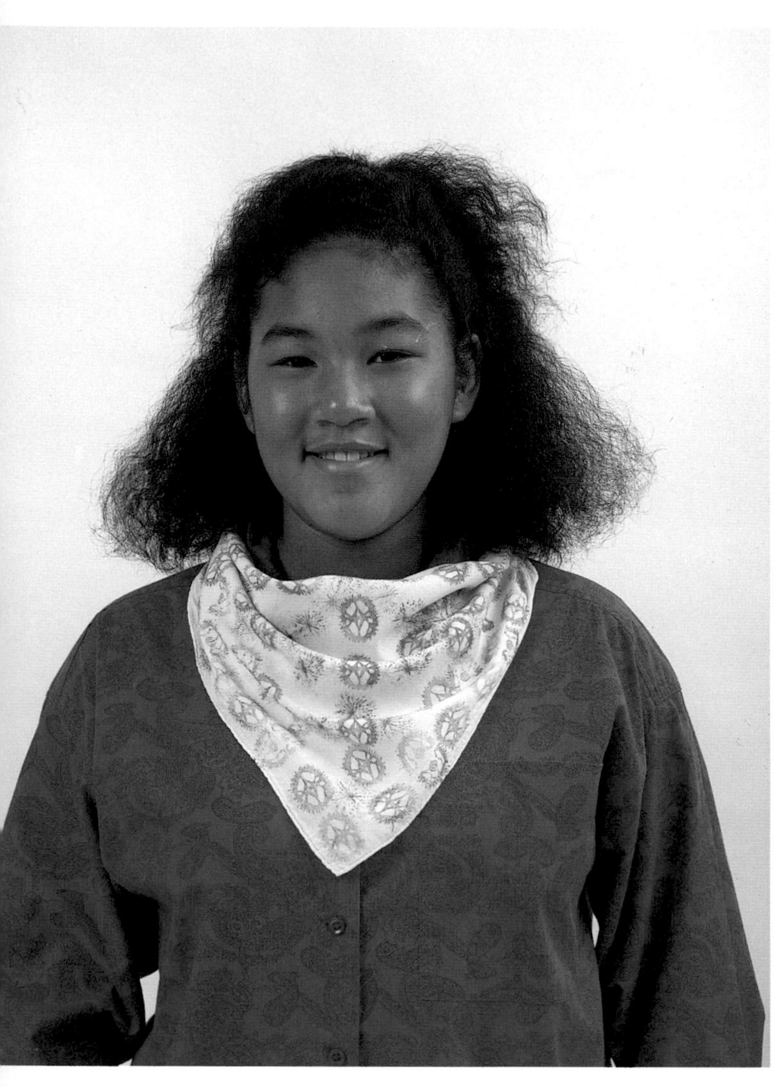

Bandanna

What You'll Need

- A walnut or other nut
- A white or solid-colored handkerchief about 18 inches square
- An iron
- Newspaper
- Old rags or a piece of foam
- An ink pad

What to Do

1. Get an adult to help you cut the walnut across the middle—opposite to the way it would normally split. (A hammer and chisel will work.) Cut one of the halves in half again. Get all the meat out of the inside and make sure the outside is clean. You may need a toothpick and an old toothbrush to get all the meat out.
2. Fold the handkerchief in half several times, until it's about 3 inches square. Iron the folded handkerchief well, and when you unfold it, the crease marks will form squares. Use this grid to help keep your design symmetrical over the whole hanky.
3. Place newspapers over a layer of old rags or a piece of foam rubber, to create a soft surface. Open the handkerchief and lay it out on the newspaper.
4. Using the creases as guidelines, begin making your design. Press the nutshell firmly into the stamp pad and then onto the handkerchief. (You may want to practice a few times on scratch paper first.) Work out from the center. Use all sides of the shell—the half, the quarter, and the outside.

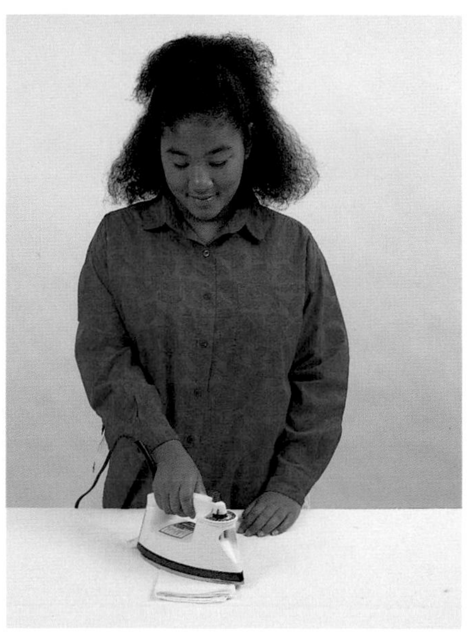

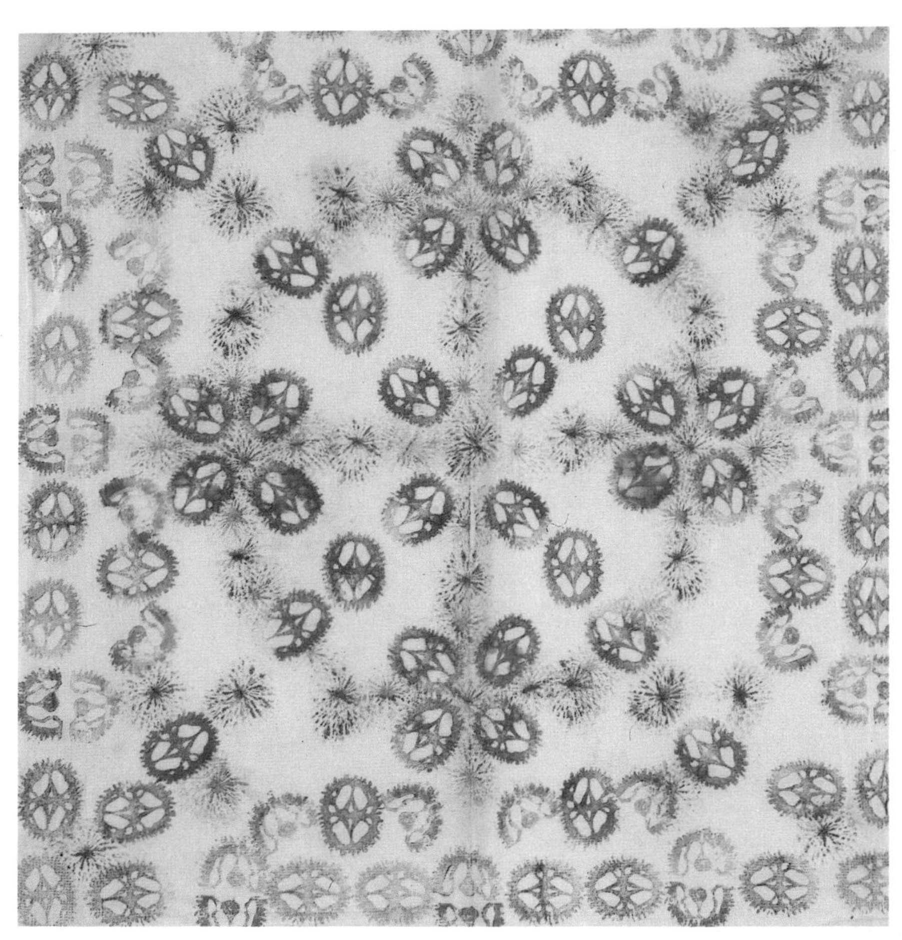

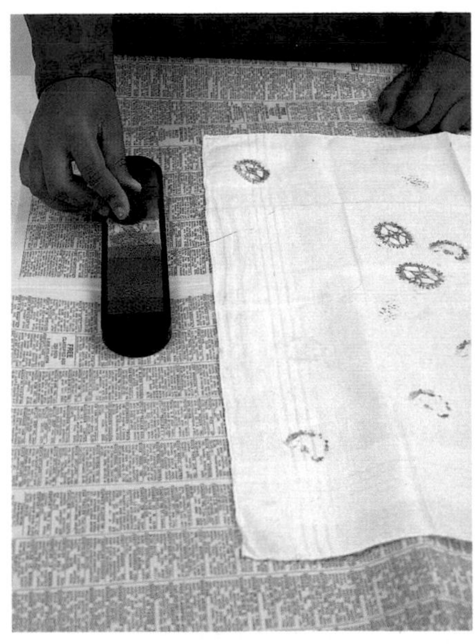

Apple Monsters

What You'll Need

- ■ A large apple
- ■ A paring knife
- ■ A wooden craft stick (like the ones found in Popsicles)
- ■ Two cloves
- ■ A few grains of uncooked rice
- ■ A sock
- ■ Scissors
- ■ White glue

What to Do

1. Carefully peel the skin off the apple, leaving a small circle of skin at the stem end. Push a craft stick into the bottom.

2. Carve a dent for each eye, and a nose.

3. Carve a slit for the mouth.

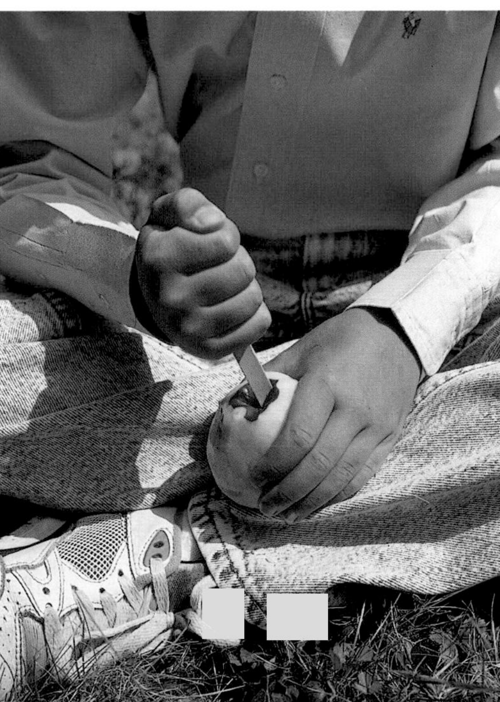

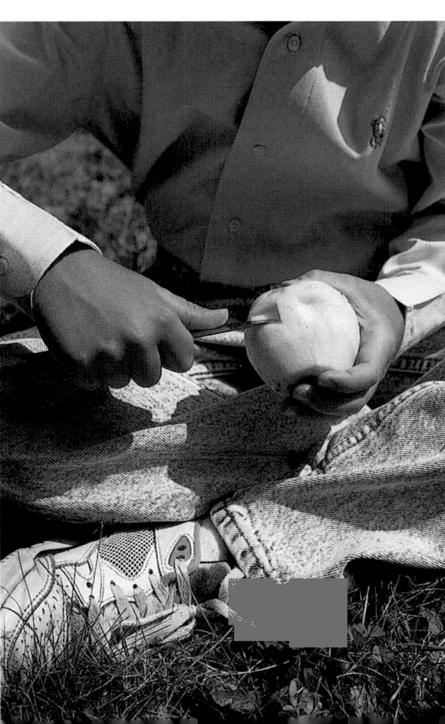

4. Push a clove into each eye socket. Push grains of rice into the area on top of and below the mouth slit for teeth.

5. Set the apple in a warm, dry place for a couple of weeks. Check it OFTEN to be sure it doesn't rot.

If the place is too damp, the apple will begin to get green spots. If this happens, try putting the apple in a warm oven (200 degrees F.) with the door slightly open for an hour. That will hasten the drying.

6. As the apple dries, you can squeeze it and mold it into a face that you like. The apple will get harder and harder and smaller and smaller as it dries.

7. When the apple is dry, make a body for it, using a sock. Cut a small hole in the toe for the craft stick to go through, and a hole on either side of the toe for your fingers to stick out and be the puppet's arms. Decorate the sock with fabric paint, or glue on decorations. You can also add yarn hair, or make a hat from a ring cut from the ankle end of the sock.

You can hold onto the craft stick with three fingers and stick the other two out of the holes.

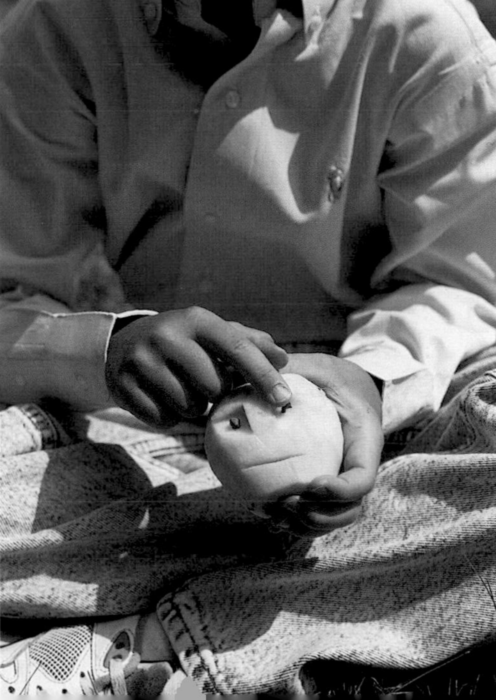

Corn Husk Flowers

What You'll Need

- Corn husks
- Fabric dye (optional)
- Flexible wire (the spool kind)
- Scissors
- Stiff, heavy wire for the stem
- Floral tape

What to Do

1. Corn husks are sold in some craft stores. Or you can shuck your own. Just peel the husks off several ears of

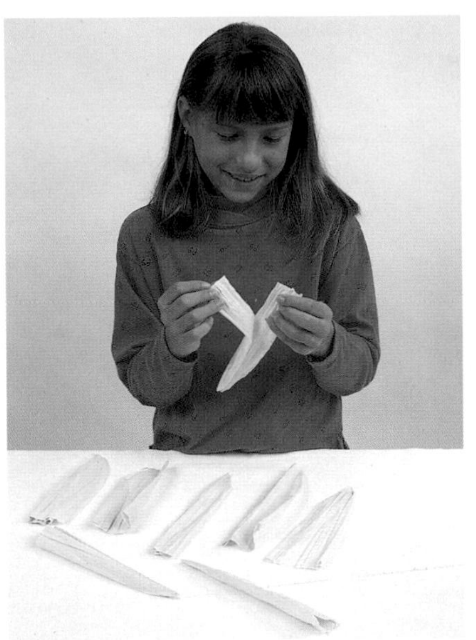

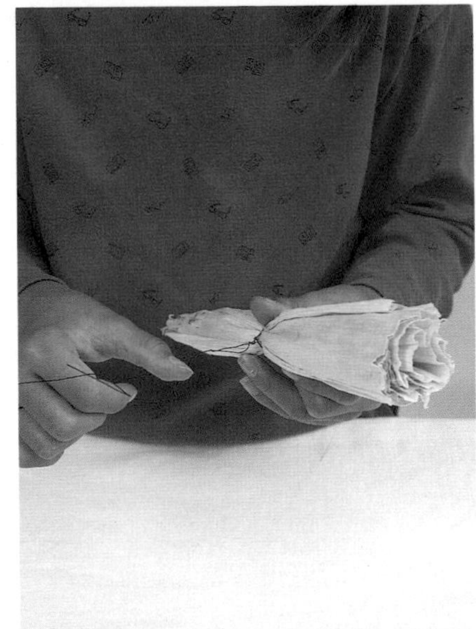

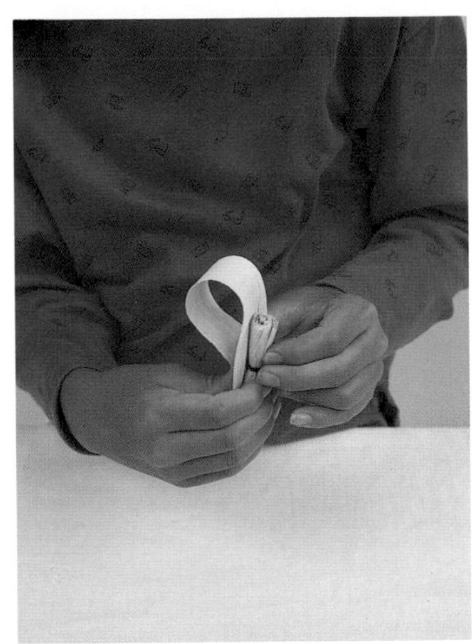

corn and spread the husks in the sun to dry, turning them every few hours.

2. Husks look good left their natural color, but you can also dye them bright colors. Get an adult to help you with this step. Dissolve about half a package of fabric dye (available in most grocery stores) in half a gallon of water, and heat to boiling. Put the dry husks in the hot dye, remove the dye from the heat, and let the husks soak overnight, or until they are the color you want.

2. Tear your husks lengthwise into strips. You'll need 5 good strips about 1-3/4 inches wide for the petals.

3. Use your less attractive husks to make the center of the flower. Roll the husks into a roll about 3/4 inch wide, and wrap flexible wire around them about an inch from one end. Cut off the wire ends and the extra husk.

4. Fold a petal in half, and position it against the center. Wrap a piece of wire around the center and the petal, twist the ends together, and trim off the wire ends. Then add the other petals around the center in the same way.

5. Cut off the extra husks on the bottom of the flower, cutting the bottom into a point.

6. Cut a piece of heavy wire about 18 inches long, and bend a "fish hook" into one end. Insert the other end into the center of the flower and pull it all the way in, until the fish hook disappears into the flower.

7. Wrap floral tape around the base of the flower and all the way down the stem. Green floral tape is sold in craft stores. It sticks to itself (or anything else) when it's stretched, so pull on it as you wrap.

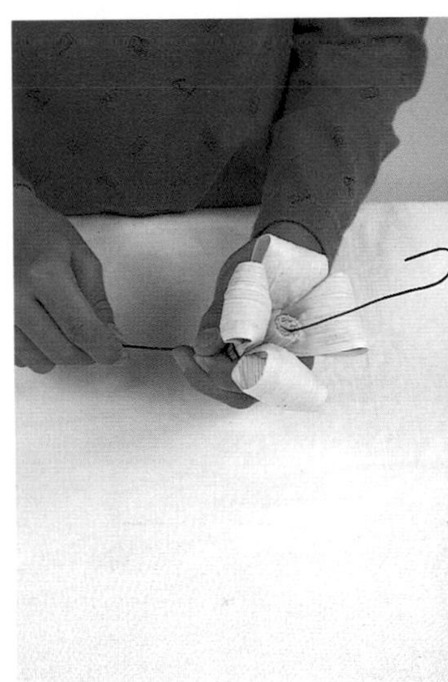

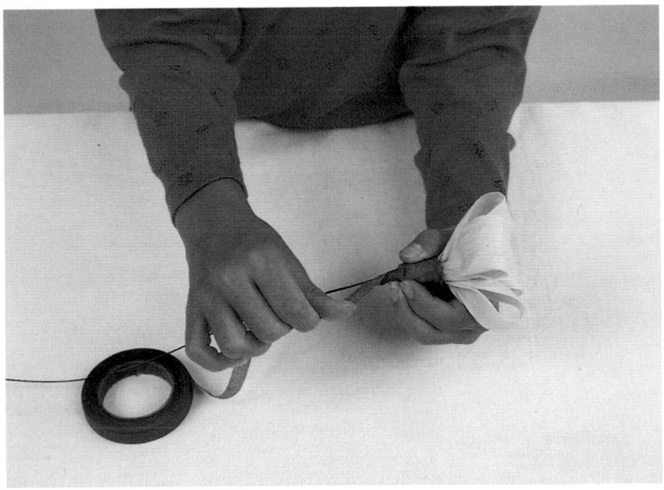

Turnip Lanterns

What You'll Need

- The largest turnip you can find
- A sharp paring knife
- A teaspoon
- String
- Scissors
- A small tea candle or a very short (1–2 inch) end of a regular-sized candle
- An awl or large nail

What to Do

1. Carving a turnip is something like carving a pumpkin except that the skin is softer and there are no seeds in the inside. The inside can be tough, however. To start out, cut a slice off of the top (stem end) of the turnip; then make a series of cuts about an inch deep into the meat of the turnip.

2. When you have made a number of cuts, try wiggling some of the pieces out with the knife or scooping them

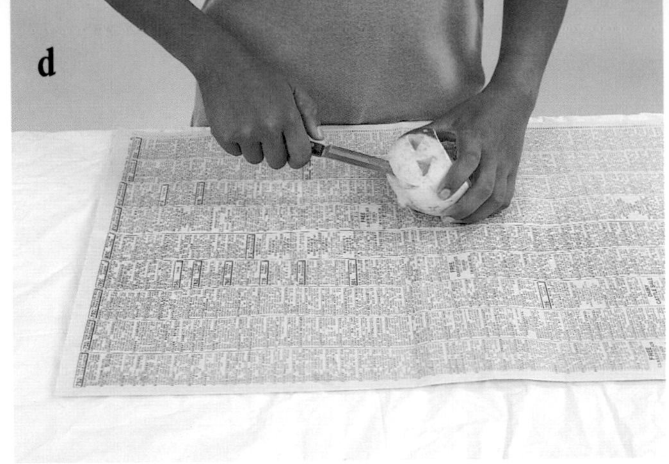

out with the spoon. If you are still having trouble getting any pieces out, make more and perhaps deeper cuts. Eventually you should be able to scoop out a shallow hole.

3. Now take the knife and cut a circle around the inside edge, and continue to make deep, short cuts to loosen the next layer of meat. Again, when you have made a number of cuts, scoop out the meat. Continue with this process until the inside is hollowed out. Be careful not to cut too close to the wall or the bottom.

4. Select the side that you want to put the face on, and carve the face. Stick the paring knife into the turnip at an angle aiming away from the hole you are cutting.

Continue making cuts like this one all around the eyes, nose, and mouth. You can get fancy and add eyebrows if you have a big enough turnip.

5. With the awl or nail, poke three holes for the strings, on either side of the eyes and directly in back of the face. Tie a piece of string 12 inches long in each hole; then tie the 3 ends together.

6. Place the little candle inside the turnip. Hang the turnip in a window with the candle lit and watch the spooky shadows dance!

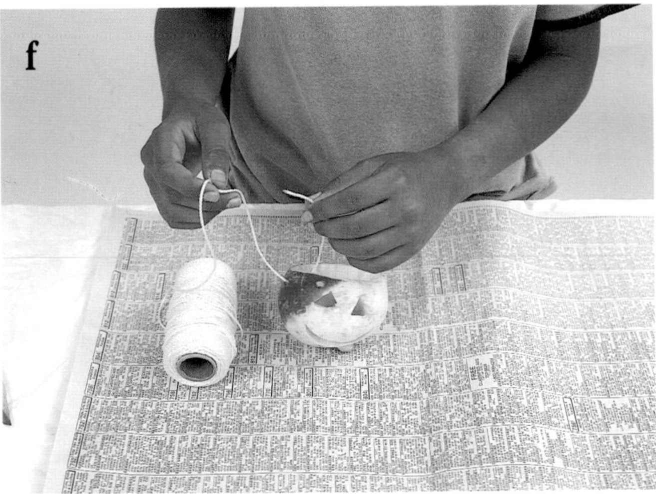

Casts of Animal Tracks

What You'll Need

- ■ Quick-drying plaster of Paris
- ■ A plastic container for mixing
- ■ A spoon
- ■ A container of water
- ■ Petroleum jelly
- ■ A strip of posterboard about 18 inches long and 2 inches wide
- ■ 2 paper clips
- ■ A trowel
- ■ A plastic dishpan, or some other container

What to Do

1. Find an animal track.
2. Carefully clear away any leaves, sticks, or stones around the track. Be careful not to touch it.
3. Put some plaster of Paris in the plastic container and slowly add water, stirring as you pour. Add water and stir until the plaster is the consistency of thick cream.
4. Cover one side of the posterboard strip with petroleum jelly. Bend the strip into a ring, with the jelly on the inside. Make the ring the size you want your finished cast to be. Clip the ring together with the paper clip, and put the ring on top of the animal track.
5. Pour the plaster of Paris into the ring until the track is covered by at least an inch of plaster. Bend the second paper clip in half and set it on top of the plaster, to use as a hook for hanging the cast on the wall.
6. Leave the cast for at least 30 minutes to set up. Then use the trowel to carefully dig around the cast. Don't try to clean it off yet. Dig up some soil with the cast so you don't gouge the plaster, which won't be quite hard yet. Place it in the dishpan to carry home.
7. Let the cast set up overnight. Then remove the paper ring and brush off the loose soil. Hang it up by the paper clip hook.

ANIMAL TRACKS

Most wild animals are shy and afraid of people. Many come out only at night or in the very early morning when humans are sleeping. You may never see them, but you know they're around by the tracks they leave behind. Figuring out what kind of animal made the tracks can be a lot of fun.

A good first step is to count the number of toes and claws in a footprint. That's usually enough to tell you the general type of animal.

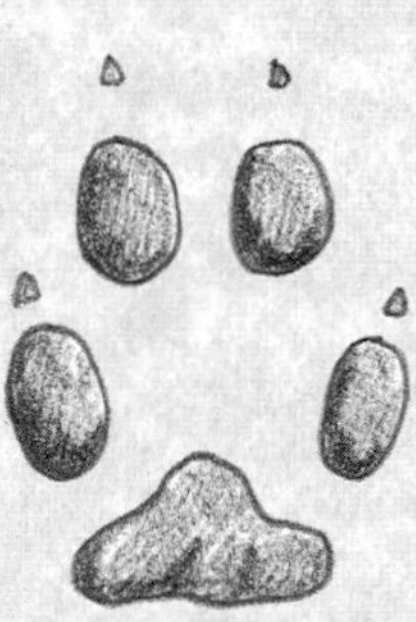

Members of the dog family (dogs, foxes, wolves, and coyotes) leave tracks that have four toes in the front footprint and four in the rear footprint, and you can usually see claw marks.

Members of the cat family (bobcat, lynx, mountain lion, and ordinary house cat) also have four toes front and rear. But cats pull their claws in when they walk, so they don't leave claw marks.

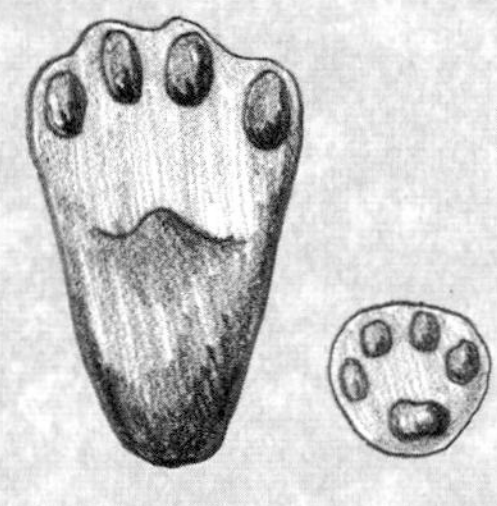

Rabbits, too, have four toes up front and in back, and sometimes you can see claws. But the real giveaway is the size of their feet: The back feet are two to three times bigger than the front!

Most mice, rats and other rodents (chipmunks, squirrels, woodchucks, beavers, and muskrats) have four toes in front and five in back. The toes are usually spread out like a fan or hand.

Animals that make tracks with five toes front and rear, with claw marks, are usually members of the weasel family (skunks, otters, badgers, minks, weasels, and wolverines).

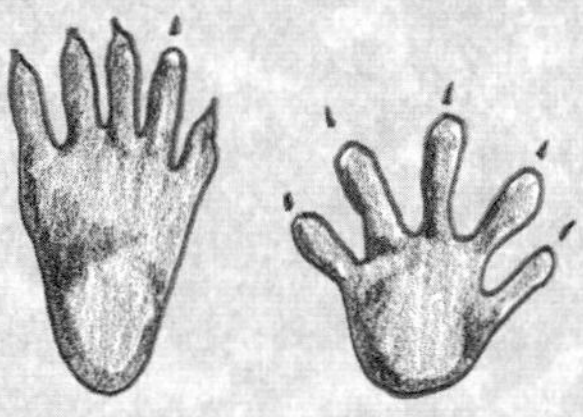

But if those clawed, five-toed tracks remind you a little of a human foot or hand, they were probably made by a bear, raccoon, or opossum.

All hoofed animals (deer, cows, moose, sheep, mountain goats) make prints with two large "toes" side by side. An exception is the horse, which leaves upside-down, U-shaped prints: the outline of the horseshoes nailed to its hooves.

THE TRACKER

When Tom Brown, Jr. was eight years old, he began to learn tracking from an 83-year-old Apache Indian named Stalking Wolf. The more time Tom spent in the woods learning the traditional Native American ways to read animal signs, the more drawn into tracking he became. He would spend hours on his belly studying tracks. In fact, he spent so much time crawling on the ground that he developed a callus—an extra layer of tough skin—across his lower chest!

Stalking Wolf taught Tom that each track tells a story, and helped him learn how to see tracks even on bare rock! Today, Tom Brown, Jr. is known far and wide as "The Tracker." Police departments call on him often to help them find criminals or lost hikers. He is considered the best tracker in the country. From a single footprint, he can tell not only whether a person is a man or woman, boy or girl, but also the person's weight and height, whether they're left-handed or right-handed, and even whether they've eaten recently.

Tom has written many books about tracking, and runs a tracking and wilderness survival school in which he has taught thousands of people. "Every mark is a track," Tom teaches. "Every dent, scrape, every rolling hill, every scratch is a track. The Grand Canyon is a water track. A fallen tree is a track of the disease that killed it and the wind that knocked it over. The ground is an open book. It is littered with tracks, from the largest to the smallest, and each one tells you something."

Most of all, Tom wants people to understand that learning how to track animals is a way to become closer to all of nature. "You don't have to follow an animal very far," he says, "before you realize that its tracks are connected to the tracks of everything else, including your own tracks. You begin to see the web of life."

WALK LIKE A BEAR

One way to "read" animal tracks is to study how different animals walk. Each walking style makes a particular pattern of tracks on the ground.

The best way to learn the patterns is to practice how different animals move. Get down on all fours and pretend you're an animal. Your hands are front feet and your knees are rear feet. (It's best to do this on soft ground or sand, so you can see the track patterns you make.)

Now "walk" by moving your right front foot and your left rear foot at the same time . . . then your left front foot and your right rear foot . . . and so on. That's how all cats, dogs, and hoofed animals (such as deer) move when they travel at normal speed. They're known as diagonal or perfect walkers. They make a nearly straight, left-foot, right-foot pattern of tracks.

Now try another one. Move your right front and right rear feet at the same time, then your left front and left rear feet, and so on. Now you're walking like a bear. Bears and other wide-bodied animals (such as porcupines, raccoons, opossums, and beavers) are pacers, or imperfect walkers. They sort of waddle when they walk and leave a close, zigzag pattern. Often, one side's

front print is almost directly across from the other side's rear print.

Bounders include most members of the weasel family. They more or less bounce from one place to another. To imitate a bounder, move both your front feet forward at the same time with a kind of lunging motion, then quickly bring your rear feet up just behind the front feet. Then move the front feet forward again, then the rear, etc. Bounders make an evenly spaced, boxlike pattern, with right and left paw prints pretty much side by side.

Rabbits and most rodents, including squirrels, are hoppers. They move by jumping ahead with their rear feet, coming down on their front feet, and then pulling their rear feet in front of and to either side of the forefeet to push off again. Few people are nimble enough to do this as gracefully as a rabbit, but you can try. Ready? Reach out with your front "feet," then bring your knees up ahead of and to the outside of your arms. You probably won't be able to push off with your rear feet (actually, your knees), but you'll get the idea.

BIGFOOT TRACKS?

Tom Steenburg tracks bigger game than cats and squirrels. A Canadian who lives in Water Valley, Alberta, Steenburg searches for the footprints of a huge, furry, manlike creature known as the Sasquatch, or Bigfoot. No one, including Steenburg, is sure that such a creature exists. In fact, most scientists laugh at the whole idea of an eight-foot-tall giant roaming around Canada and the American Northwest.

But hundreds of people claim to have caught a glimpse of Bigfoot, and people have been finding huge, human-like footprints for over a hundred years. Whenever Steenburg finds a huge footprint, he makes a plaster cast of it. And while many people laugh, no one can explain how those footprints got there.

WINTER

Snow Candles

What You'll Need

- Snow
- Paraffin or beeswax
- A tin can
- A pan
- Old crayons or old colored candles
- Candle wicking*
- Waxed paper
- A stick
- An oven mitt

*Candle wicking is sold in craft stores.

What to Do

1. Get an adult to help you with this step. Place the paraffin or beeswax in the tin can. Pour 2 inches of water into the pan, and add the can of paraffin. Heat the pan on the stove until the water boils, then turn the burner down so that the water simmers but doesn't boil. Carefully watch the paraffin as it melts. Stir in old crayons or old pieces of colored candles if you want your snow candles to have color.

Never put paraffin directly in a pan over the burner. The paraffin may catch fire if you do. Always use the double boiler method described here.

2. As soon as the wax melts, turn off the stove. Dip the candle wicking in the melted wax, so that it is fairly stiff. Lay it out straight on a piece of waxed paper to dry.

3. Go outside to prepare the snow mold. Find a spot where the snow is at least a foot deep and cold and dry enough to hold its shape when you poke a hole in it.

4. Use a stick to poke a hole a few inches deep in the snow. This will be your candle mold. Experiment with different shapes of holes. When you are satisfied with the shape, go back inside and turn the stove on again. It won't take long for the water to get hot again and for the wax to melt if it has hardened a bit.

5. Using an oven mitt or hot pad, carry the can of melted wax and the piece of candle wicking outside to the snow mold. Dangle the wick down the center of the mold, and carefully pour the melted wax around the wick into the hole. Hold onto the wick for a few minutes until the wax cools and hardens enough to hold the wick straight.

6. Let the candle cool for about an hour.

SNOW

A snowflake is actually a bunch of ice crystals stuck together. The life of an ice crystal begins two to six miles up in the sky, when a tiny droplet of water freezes around a speck of dust, bacteria, or another ice crystal. Then the new crystal starts to fall.

The crystal's shape depends on the temperature and the amount of water in the air. As it falls through the sky, it changes shape constantly—with every slight change in air temperature or moisture, every little breeze. Sometimes it changes completely, other times only a little. A flat, straight-sided crystal may suddenly sprout "arms." A beautiful snow "star" may lose its points, and then grow spiny needles at one end.

Even the slight differences in temperature and moisture from one side of a crystal to the other make the two sides different.

That's why most scientists believe that the chances of two snow crystals being exactly alike are slim. Each one is created by its own special miniature "climate," by the exact conditions it falls through from one second to the next—and even by the way it falls.

7. Carefully dig the candle out of the hole by digging around it with your hands. Bring the candle inside and rinse it off under cool water.

8. Trim the wick to about an inch. Carefully trim or scrape off any bumps on the bottom of the candle so it will stand up.

9. Make an arrangement for a table or mantle by cutting a few evergreen branches and using them to surround the base of the candle. Try nestling several candles in some evergreen branches.

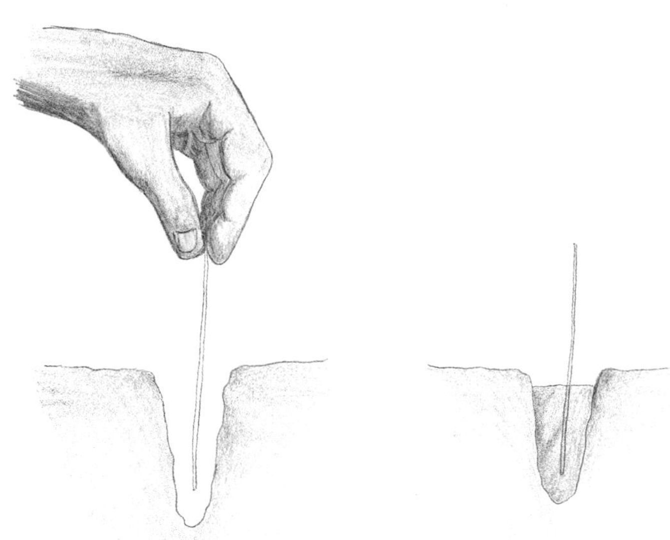

Every time it flutters, turns over, or bumps into another crystal, it changes shape.

Before it reaches the ground, an ice crystal may fall for as long as two hours and may travel hundreds of miles. Usually, somewhere along the way it catches onto a little puff of other crystals joined together—a snowflake. Finally, it floats to earth, along with trillions of other snowflakes.

KINDS OF SNOW

Generally, there are three types of fresh snow. There's dry, fluffy snow—the kind that floats down from the sky like big feathers. It's made mostly of snow "stars" from low, cold clouds.

There's wet snow, the sort that's extra good for making snowballs and snow people. Its crystals look like flat, six-sided plates, and come from low, fairly warm clouds.

Also, there's fine, dry, powdery snow—the kind that looks like sugar and blows in the wind with a soft, hissing sound. It's made up of tiny crystals shaped like discs or pegs from high, very cold clouds.

Snow Sculpture

What You'll Need

- Snow (slushy snow works best, like the snow on a warmish day after a snowfall)
- Heavy, waterproof gloves
- A small hatchet
- A hammer
- A wide chisel

What to Do

1. Decide what to make and where you want it to be. Remember that white snow shows up better against a dark background, such as some evergreen bushes or trees, or against a brick wall or in a dark building.
2. Decide how big you want your sculpture to be—probably no taller than you are. Start with simple shapes, such as a snow person, an elephant, a bear, a house, a whale, etc.
3. Begin by making large snow boulders. To do this, roll hard-packed snowballs along the snowy ground until the boulder is as large as you can lift. It helps to roll in the direction of your building site, so you won't have to carry the boulder as far.
4. When your boulders are next to each other, stack them in the general shape of the finished figure—a pyramid, for example, a rectangle, or a square.

5. When your boulders are arranged, start smoothing them into the shape of the figure. Add smaller boulders and snowballs to fill out the figure. Scoop away snow that you don't need. If the snow gets hard, use the hatchet to hack away unwanted snow.

6. Keep in mind that the bottom is the weakest part of the sculpture, and shore it up with more snow if it seems to weaken or begins to cave in while you are working.

7. After you've built the general shape, begin to add details. You can use the end of a twig to add fine lines. If the snow has gotten hard, use the hammer and chisel carefully to chip way small areas. Some people like to use objects in their sculptures, such as pine cones, twigs, carrots, etc.

8. Be sure to photograph your sculpture if you want to keep it!

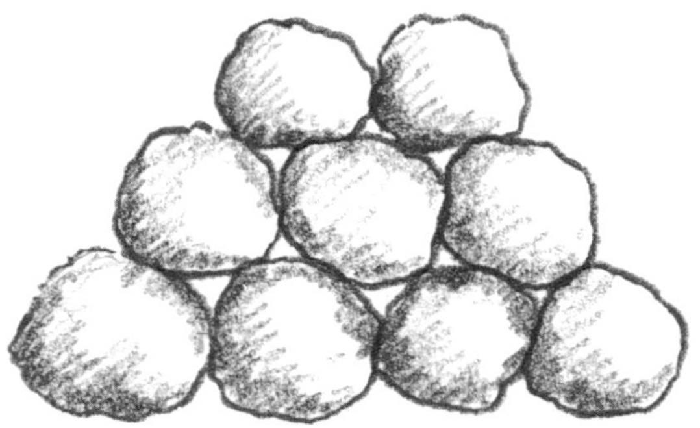

SNOW FACTS

■ One inch of rain would make about 10 inches of snow.

■ There are about one million ice crystals in a patch of snow two feet wide, two feet long, and 10 inches deep.

■ The odds of two ice crystals being exactly alike: one in 105,000,000 (that's 10 to the five millionth power) .

■ The greatest snowfall in one day (24 hours): 76 inches—over six feet—on April 14 to 15, 1921, in Silver Lake, Colorado.

■ The greatest snowfall in one year: 1,224 inches—that's 102 feet— at the Paradise Ranger Station, Mt. Rainier, Washington, between February 19, 1971 and February 18, 1972.

SNOW FOLKLORE

■ When hornets build their nests higher than usual, expect a snowy winter.

■ When a dog howls at the moon in winter it is a sign of snow.

■ If snow begins in mid of day,
Expect a foot of it to lay.

■ The day of the month of the season's first snowfall is the number of days it will snow that winter.

■ Put a pint of snow from the season's first snowfall on a stove and slowly melt it. The number of bubbles that rise to the surface is the number of snowfalls to expect.

■ Large flakes at first, the storm will last.
Small flakes at first, it'll be over fast.

THE SNOWFLAKE MAN

In 1880, when Wilson Bentley was 15 years old, his mother showed him a microscope. It changed his life forever.

The Vermont farm boy became fascinated with looking at things under the microscope. Most interesting of all were snowflakes. He spent hours gazing through his microscope at snowflakes he collected as they fell. At first, he tried to draw the shapes. But he couldn't capture the true beauty of the delicate crystals.

Then he read that it was possible to take photographs through a microscope. Wilson knew nothing about photography, but he convinced his father to buy him a camera. It took him months to learn how, but on January 15, 1885, when he was 20 years old, Wilson Bentley did it: He took the first successful "photo-micrograph" of an ice crystal.

For the next 48 years, Bentley spent his winters in a cold, open shed catching snowflakes on a velvet-lined tray and quickly photographing them. Soon he became known far and wide as the "Snowflake Man."

All together, Wilson Bentley took more than 4,500 separate ice crystal photomicrographs. In 1931, almost half of his photos were published in a now-famous book, Snow Crystals. Scientists still use it to help them study the wonder of snow.

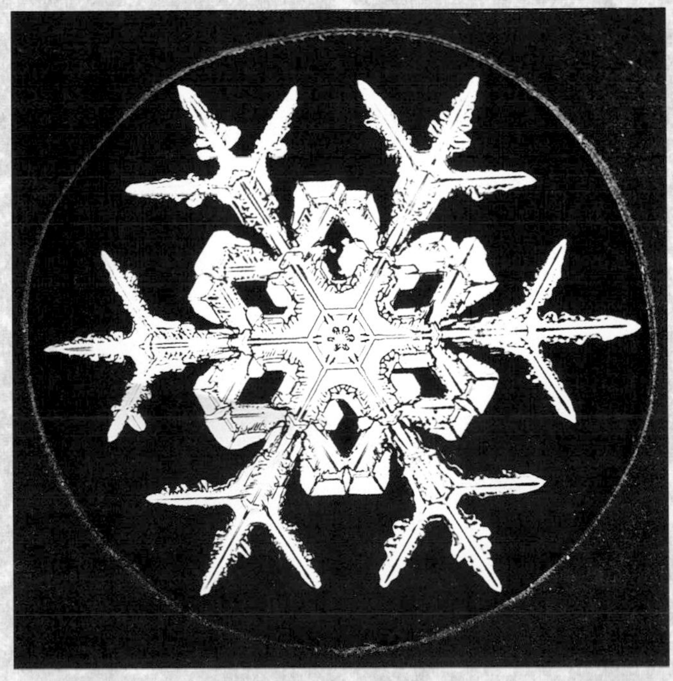

Birds' Midwinter Tree

What You'll Need

- A bag of whole cranberries or other red edible berries
- A bag of peanuts in their shells
- An apple
- A kiwi fruit
- 2 oranges
- Some whole cloves
- Some heavy cotton thread
- A needle
- Raffia* or heavy string or cord

*Raffia is available in craft stores.

What to Do

1. Make a garland of the cranberries by stringing them on a doubled length of thread. (If you want, string some popped corn with the cranberries. It will show up well if you don't have snow, and the birds like it.)
2. Push the needle through the middle of the peanuts to make a peanut garland.
3. Slice the apple, the kiwi, and one of the oranges crosswise, so that each slice has a pretty pattern. Make the slices rather thin (about 1/4 inch thick).

Put a loop of raffia or cord through the edge of each slice. Use a pointed stick or a small screwdriver to poke a hole to put the cord or raffia through.
4. Make pomanders for the birds. (They won't eat the cloves, but the pomanders will look nice on the tree.) Poke holes all over an orange with an awl or a small screwdriver, and insert small cloves.

Cut four pieces of raffia about a foot long, and tie them together about 3 inches from their ends. Put the pomander in the center, and tie the raffia together at the other end. Hang from a branch.

GUESS WHO'S COMING TO DINNER

Lots of birds like fruit, including catbirds, orioles, redwings, robins, and tanagers.

Bird Feeder

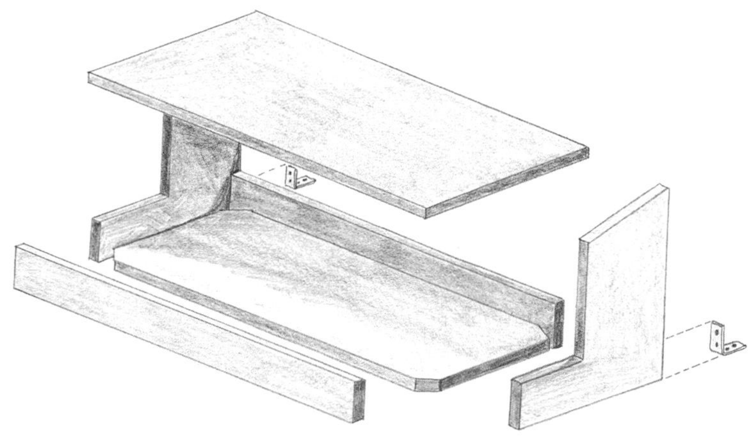

This simple feeder attaches to the outside of a window, so you can watch the birds when they drop in for dinner. Filling the feeder is a snap, too: Just open your window and pour in some seed!

The feeder looks good just painted a neutral color. If you want to make it even fancier, you can paint a design on the roof, like the ivy shown in the photograph.

If you're not used to shopping for boards or screws, ask the sales person at the hardware store to help you find the things on this list.

What You'll Need

- An 8-foot-long 1 X 12 pine or fir board (to make the top, bottom, sides, and back)
- A 2-foot-long 1 X 3 pine or fir board (for the front)

■ 16 to 20 #6 1-1/4" brass or galvanized wood screws
■ Two 1-1/2" corner brackets with screws
■ A saw
■ Sandpaper
■ A drill
■ A screwdriver
■ Boiled linseed oil
■ House paint

What to Do

1. Saw the top, bottom, side, and back parts of the feeder to the sizes shown in the drawings. (Remember the carpenter's Golden Rule: Measure twice, cut once!)
2. Sand all edges smooth.
3. Paint the top, sides, back, and front with a neutral-color latex or oil house paint. Be sure that all surfaces—both sides and the edges—of each piece are covered. *Don't* paint the feeder bottom; if you do, birds might eat bits of paint as they peck at their food.
4. Pour linseed oil onto the feeder bottom and rub it in thoroughly with a rag to protect the wood.
5. Attach the feeder back to the bottom with wood screws. Drill holes first to avoid splitting the wood.
6. Now (drilling first each time) screw on the sides . . . the front . . . and the top.
7. Give the feeder a final coat of paint, and you're done!
8. Mount the feeder to the window sill with corner brackets, as shown.

To Paint the Roof:

What You'll Need

■ A pencil
■ Ivy leaves
■ Green and brown paint pens
■ Yellow and green paint, suitable for outdoor use. (Hobby enamel or exterior latex would both work.)
■ Paint brushes, pointed
■ A narrow dowel (about 1/4 inch thick) sharpened in a pencil sharpener

What to Do

1. Find some ivy and study how it grows. Then, using a

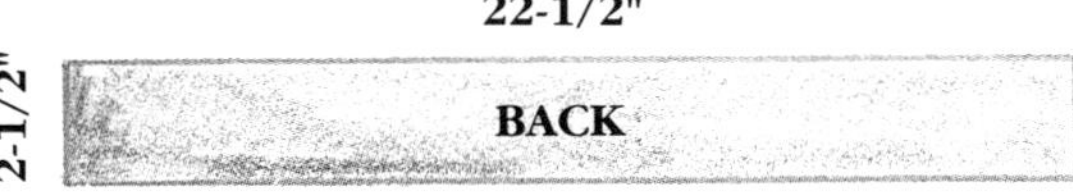

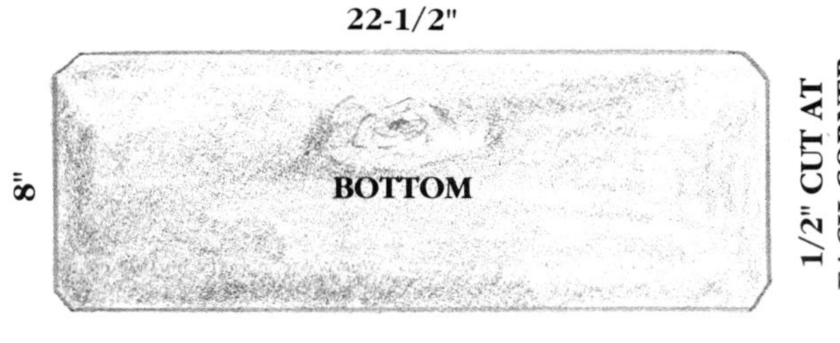

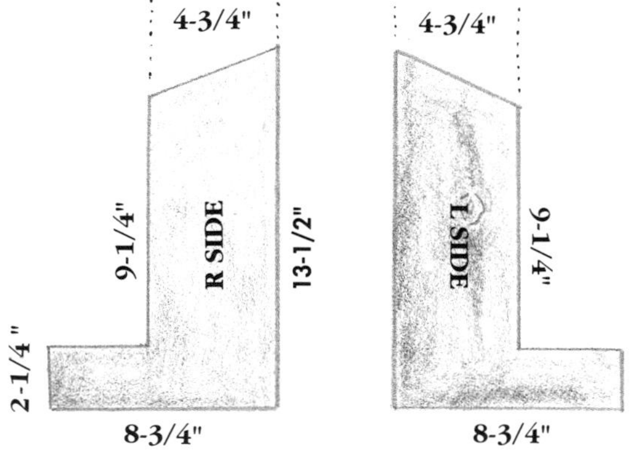

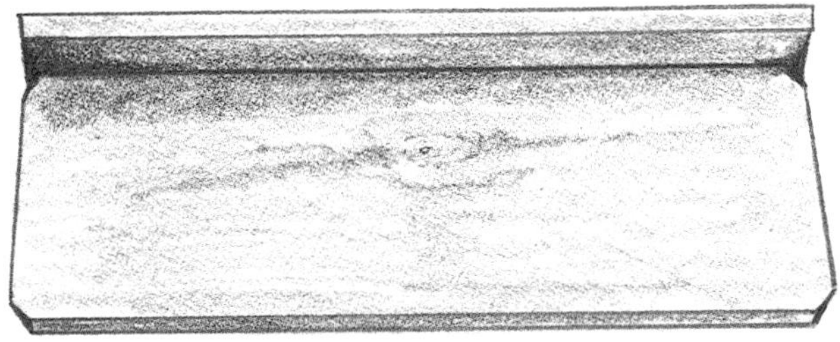

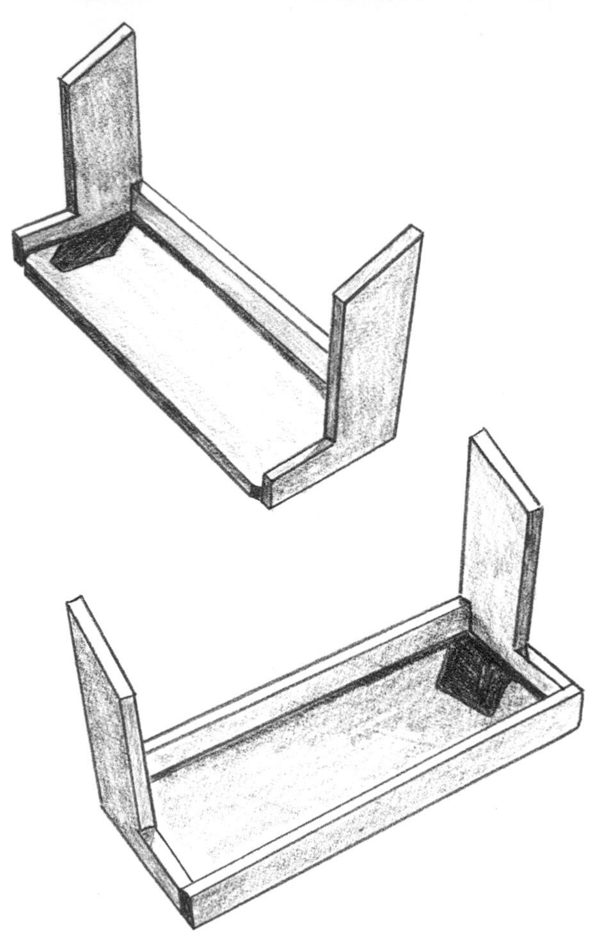

pencil, lightly sketch just a branch (no leaves) on the roof. Start with the main branch and then add the smaller branches.

2. Lay an ivy leaf a little ways away from the branch, and trace around the leaf with a pencil. Trace as many different leaves as you want, using different sizes. Use small ones at the ends of branches.

3. Sketch in the stems with a pencil.

4. With a green paint pen, go over the pencil tracings of your leaves, stems, and branches. Let dry.

5. Paint in the leaves, using green paint and a paint brush. Start at the left. Fill in one leaf, and before it's dry, use the sharpened dowel to draw in the leaf veins. (Look at the real ivy again.) If you make a mistake, just re-paint the leaf and try again.

6. Do the same for each of the leaves. As you get toward the end of the branch, mix a little yellow paint into your green paint, to make the leaves look smaller and younger.

7. Using the brown paint pen, go over the branches again. Put the brown line right underneath the green one, to look like a shadow.

WHO EATS WHAT?

Have you noticed that some birds—cardinals, for instance—spend most of their time in trees or shrubs, but others, such as robins and towhees, are usually on the ground? That's because different birds like different kinds of food. You wouldn't go to a seafood restaurant if you were hungry for pizza, right? The same is true for birds: They head for the places that serve the meals they want.

Cardinals, blue jays, and other birds with strong beaks like large berries and seeds, so they forage in holly trees, juniper bushes, and other types of vegetation that produce that sort of food. Robins are fond of earthworms, and towhees dine on crawling insects, so they peck and scratch at ground level. Sparrows and mourning doves eat small to medium seeds from tall grasses and low shrubs.

By watching where and what different birds eat in the wild, you can figure out which kinds of bird seed are most likely to attract those birds to your feeders. Just choose seeds that are similar in size and shape to the ones the birds eat from nature's menu. (Of course, some birds—such as house wrens—eat only insects. They won't come to a feeder no matter what sort of seed you offer them!)

Nearly all birds that feed in trees and bushes favor black oil-type sunflower, while seed-eating birds that forage on or near the ground are especially fond of white proso millet. Some birds are fussy about their food. The American goldfinch rejects virtually all bird foods except niger thistle and hulled sunflower seeds. Others, such as the white-throated sparrow, will try almost any seed you offer.

On the next page is a list of who eats what.

Millet: doves, sparrows.

Thistle: finches.

Safflower: cardinals, doves, sparrows.

Corn: sparrows, jays, doves.

Hulled sunflower: finches, jays, cardinals, chickadees.

Black oil sunflower: cardinals, chickadees, titmice, grosbeaks, finches.

Striped sunflower: titmice, cardinals, jays, grosbeaks.

White Proso Millet

Mixed Seeds

Niger Thistle

Safflower

Finely Cracked Corn

Hulled Sunflower

Black Oil Sunflower

Striped Sunflower

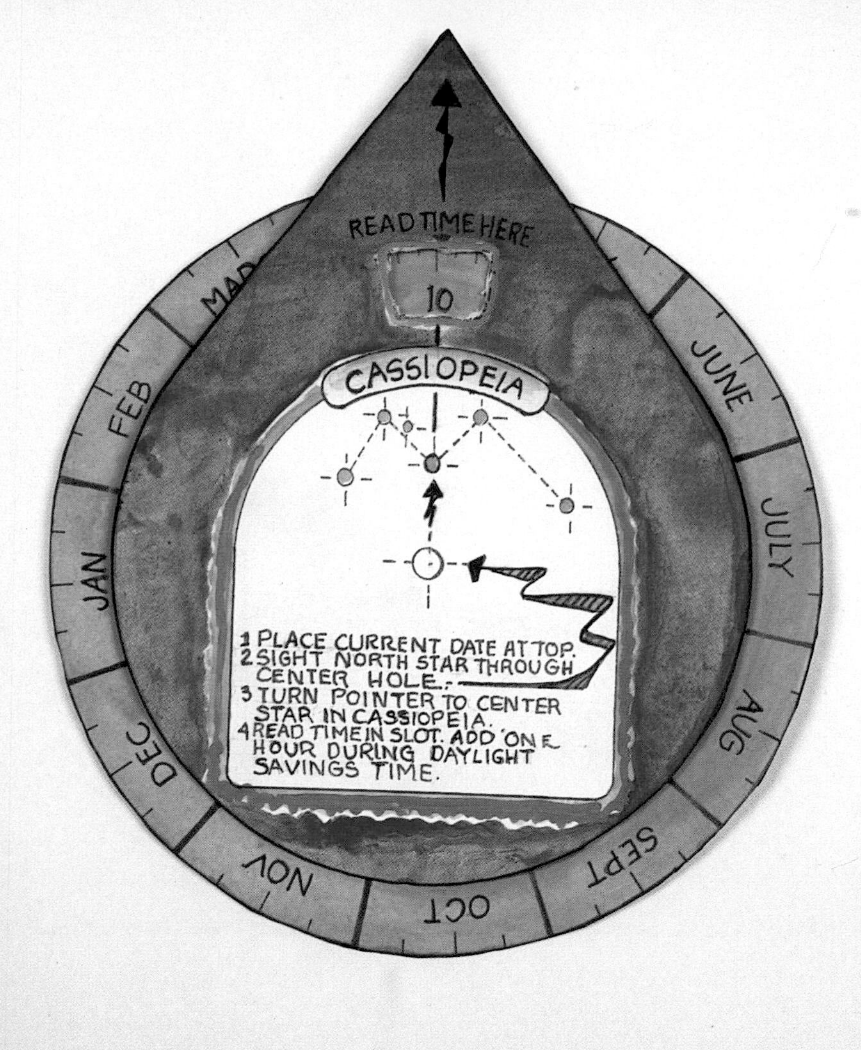

Nocturne Night Dial

With this colorful dial, you can tell time by the stars. Just turn the large outer dial so the current date is at the top, and look through the center hole at the north star. Turn the pointer to the center star in Cassiopeia, and read the time in the slot. (During Daylight Savings Time, you'll have to add one hour to the time that appears in the slot.)

What You'll Need

- Scissors
- White glue
- Posterboard
- A grommet

What to Do

1. Copy the drawings of both dials—the round one and the pointed one—on a photocopy machine.
2. Cut out the photocopied dials, and glue each one onto a piece of posterboard. Trim the posterboard to fit.
3. Color both dials with anything you like—crayons, watercolors, magic markers.
4. Cut out the slot at the top of the pointed dial.
5. Lay the pointed dial on top of the round one, so that the cut-out slot is over the circle of times. Cut a hole through the center of both dials.
6. Attach the two dials in the center with a grommet. Grommets have two important characteristics: they're hollow in the center, so you can sight through the center of the dial; and they'll allow the pointed dial to rotate. A grommet is installed with an inexpensive metal tool.

If you don't want to use a grommet, look for something else that might do the same job. For example, an audio intake valve—the kind used to attach an electric guitar to an amplifier—would also work.

HOW TO FIND THE NORTH STAR AND CASSIOPEIA

To locate the constellation Cassiopeia, you must look into the northern section of the night sky. If you don't know someone who can point this area out to you, use a compass to find true north.

Next, try to find the Big Dipper in this part of the sky. It will be near the northern horizon and is quite large. On winter evenings it will be standing on its handle, just to the right of due north. During summer evenings the Big Dipper will be to the left of due north and standing on the dipper part.

Regardless of the position of the Big Dipper, you can use it to find the North Star and Cassiopeia. The two stars that make the front edge of the dipper part are called the "pointers," and point to the North Star, which is about four times as far away from the Dipper as the pointers are apart.

Don't stop after locating the North Star. Continue along in the same direction, going an equal distance on the other side of the star until you see a group of stars that form a large zigzag W. This is the constellation Cassiopeia. It may not be right side up and may look more like an M.

You will not be able to find Cassiopeia in the evening sky from May through August, because it will be below the northern horizon. However, on clear evenings during the winter months, you will be able to see this constellation as it arcs across the northern sky.

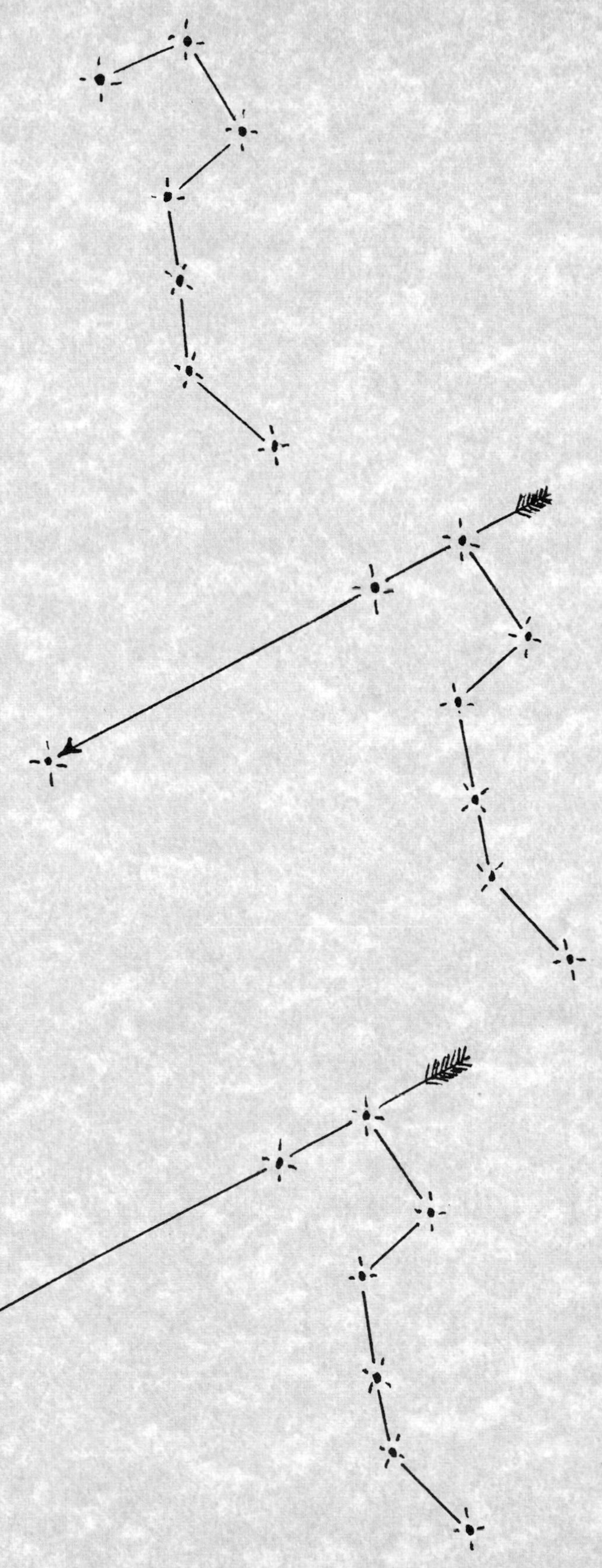

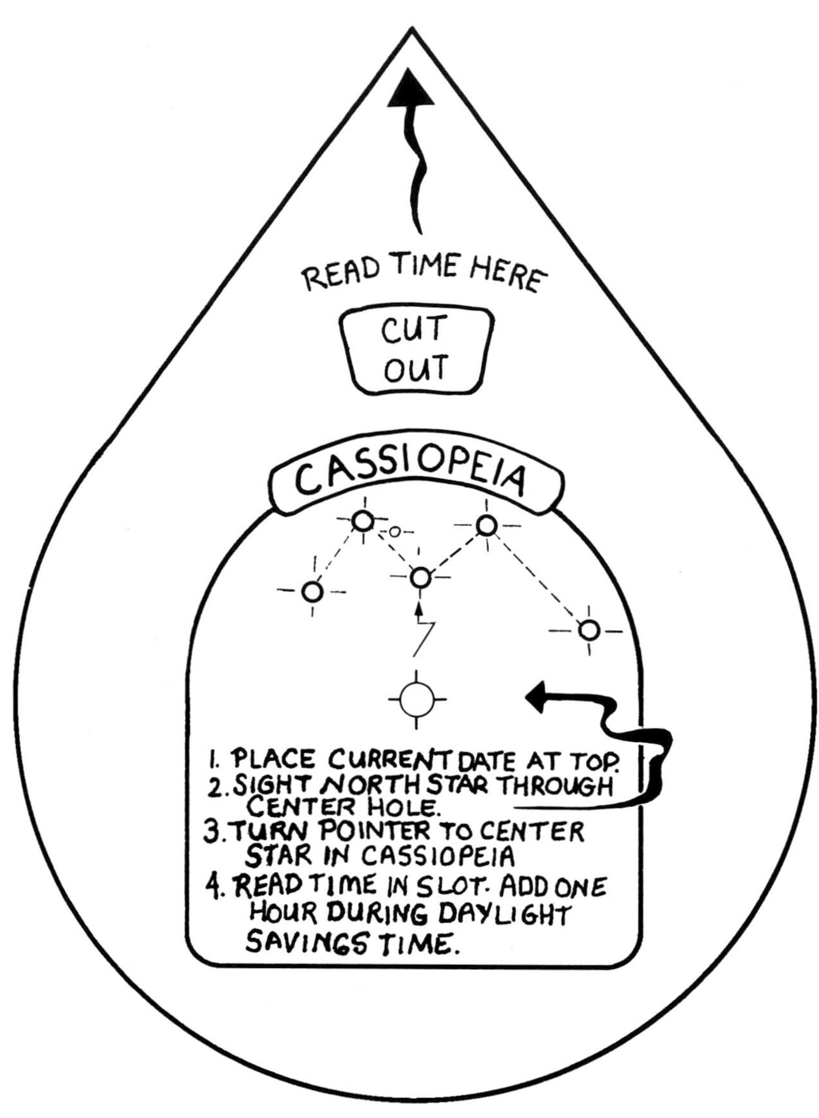

Pointed dial for Nocturne Night Dial. This one goes on top.

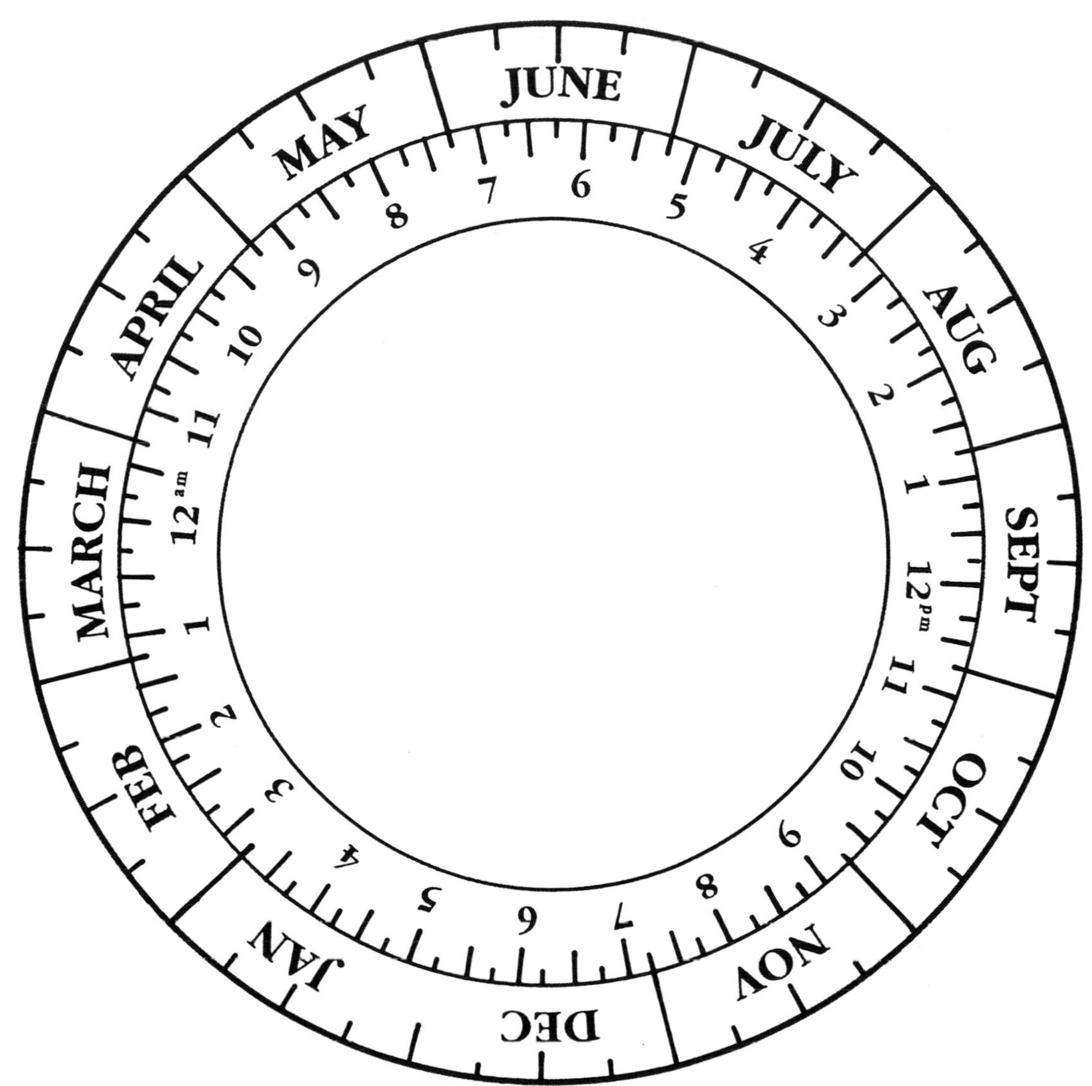

Round dial for Nocturne Night Dial. This one goes on the bottom.

Constellation Viewers

What You'll Need

- An empty can from potato chips, soup, or canned vegetables; or an empty oatmeal box; or a mailing tube
- Tracing paper
- A pencil
- Scissors
- An awl or a large nail and a hammer
- A sky map or other guide to the constellations
- Paper, glue, tape, sequins, plastic fabric paint, and other materials to cover and decorate the outside of the viewer
- A large permanent marker

What to Do

1. Remove one lid from the can or box.
2. Trace around the outside of the closed end of the can with the pencil and tracing paper.
3. Find a diagram of the constellation you want to make, and draw the dots representing stars inside the circle you have drawn on the tracing paper.
4. Turn the tracing paper over so that you can see the reverse of the constellation, and place it over the closed end of the can or box. Using the awl or large nail, hammer holes in the end of the can or box in the places where the dots representing stars are on your diagram. (If you are using an oatmeal box, you can poke the holes with the awl or nail without the hammer.)
5. Reach down into the can or box with the permanent marker, and color the entire inside of the end black. If you are using a can, you should be able to reach the end easily. (If you are using a potato chip can, you may not be able to reach the end and will have to skip this step.)
6. Now color the outside of the end of the can or box black.
7. Use paper to cover the outside of the can. Then decorate it with sequins, fabric paint, markers, or anything else that strikes your fancy.
8. To view your constellation, face a window or a light source, and hold the viewer up to your eye.

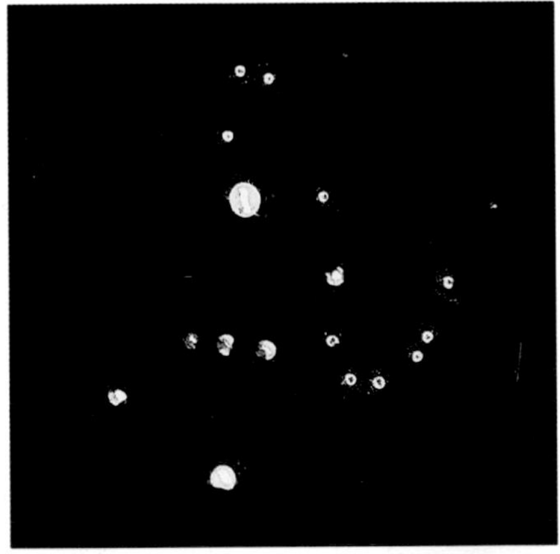

Above: The constellation Orion, from inside a constellation viewer. Opposite page: This photograph is called a star trail. The photographer pointed his camera at the night sky and left the shutter open for 12 hours. As the stars moved across the sky, they left trails of light on the film. The bright semicircle in the center is the North Star.

Bark Rubbing

What You'll Need

- A tree
- A piece of construction paper
- A piece of screening 7-1/2" by 14-1/2"
- Masking tape
- A crayon

What to Do

1. Find an interesting patch of bark, and tape the construction paper over it.
2. Holding the crayon flat side against the tree, rub up and down over the paper, pressing firmly. Keep coloring until you get an interesting pattern.
3. Remove the tape and inspect your bark rubbing. Try different trees, and look at the different patterns you get.

BARK

When most people think of trees, they think of leaves and branches. But when you're out walking in the woods, what part of the tree is closest to you? What part do you see most clearly? Not the leaves and branches. You see the trunks—and particularly the bark covering them.

Tree bark comes in all sorts of colors and textures, depending on the kind of tree. Paper birch trees are famous for their satiny, light-colored bark that peels off in strips. Some North American Indian tribes used the bark to make canoes. Maple trees have gray, shaggy bark.

Left: Maple
Right: Sycamore

Beech trees have very smooth, sleek bark. That's why beech branches look like strong, muscled arms. Sourwood bark comes in huge square blocks.

Sometimes the bark on a tree's branches looks different from the bark on its trunk. That's because the trunk is the oldest part of the tree, so its bark tends to be thicker, darker, or more deeply furrowed.

You can identify some trees just by the color of their bark. For instance, you can tell a sycamore tree from a long way off by its crazy-quilt patches of light and dark. Sweet cherry trees have deep red bark with thin black stripes circling the trunk. And the bark of a young striped maple is bright green with white up-and-down stripes!

A tree's bark is its protective outer "skin." Just beneath is the inner bark, which carries nourishing sap to feed the tree and supply energy to its roots. The bark of some trees, such as birches, really is as thin as skin. Redwood trees, though, have bark as much as a foot thick. And the bark of a giant sequoia tree can be two feet thick!

Left: Mountain Laurel
Right: Sourwood

Twig Weaving

What You'll Need

- ■ A forked tree branch
- ■ Yarn or string
- ■ Raffia,* long grasses, or more string
- ■ Any of these: feathers, seedpods, long strips of bark, moss, seashells

*Raffia is sold in craft stores.

What to Do

1. Tie one end of the yarn to the top of one of the forks of the branch.
2. Stretch the yarn across to the other fork, and wrap it around once.
3. Stretch the yarn back across to the first fork, about 1/4 inch below the first wrap (where the knot is). Wrap the yarn around.
4. Continue taking the yarn back and forth between the forks, wrapping it each time, until you reach the bottom of the fork.
5. Now weave the other materials up and down through the yarn. Go over one strand of yarn, then under the next, then over, and so on.
6. Between the strands of yarn place seashells, mosses, or other things too short to weave.

Another idea: Try using a branch with more than one fork. The large weaving pictured has three forks—and is shaped sort of like a baseball mitt.

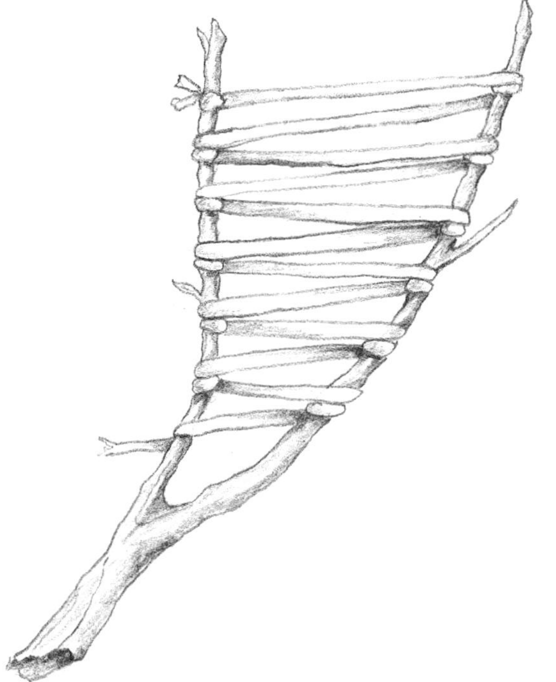

Gee-Haw Whimmy Diddle

What You'll Need

- A dead branch with several forks
- Hand clippers
- A pocket knife
- An awl
- A very small drill (also known as a pin vise)
- An 18-gauge wire brad or escutcheon pin 3/4 inch long*

*Brads and nails come in various "gauges," or widths.

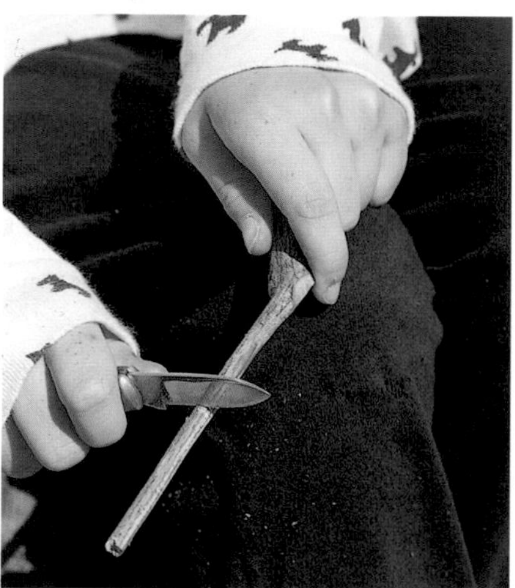

What to Do

1. With your hand clippers, cut a off a piece of the branch, so that you have a short piece for the handle and a longer piece about 1/4 inch in diameter. (A handle isn't essential; a whimmy diddle can be a perfectly straight twig. But the handle makes it easier to work.)
2. Scrape the bark off the twig with your pocket knife.
3. Trim off the ragged edges of the twig with your knife.
4. Cut off the whimmy diddle so it's about 5 or 6 inches long, and round off the end a little.
5. Cut 7 to 9 shallow notches.
6. With the awl or a nail, make a dent in the center of the end. Then use the pin vise to drill a hole about 3/4 inch deep into the end.
7. Now make the propeller. Cut a small piece of twig about 1-1/2 inches long (the end you cut off the whimmy diddle will be perfect). Scrape the bark off the propeller.
8. About 1/4 inch from each end, cut a ring around the propeller.
9. Carve the wood out between the rings, to make the propeller flat.
10. With a ruler, find the center of the propeller, and drill a hole that's just slightly bigger than the brad you're going to attach the propeller with.
11. Attach the propeller by nailing the brad into the hole.
12. Go back to the branch, cut yourself a rubbing stick, and scrape the bark off it.

How to Whimmy Diddle

1. To make the whimmy diddle *gee* (spin to the right), hold the rubbing stick in your right hand and crook your forefinger over it. As you rub the stick up and down the notches, let your forefinger rub down the far side of the whimmy.
2. To make it *haw* (spin to the left), move your hand forward so that your forefinger doesn't touch the notched stick but your thumb rubs against the near side of the whimmy diddle as you rub up and down the notches.
3. These directions are for a right-handed person. A lefty would do just the opposite.

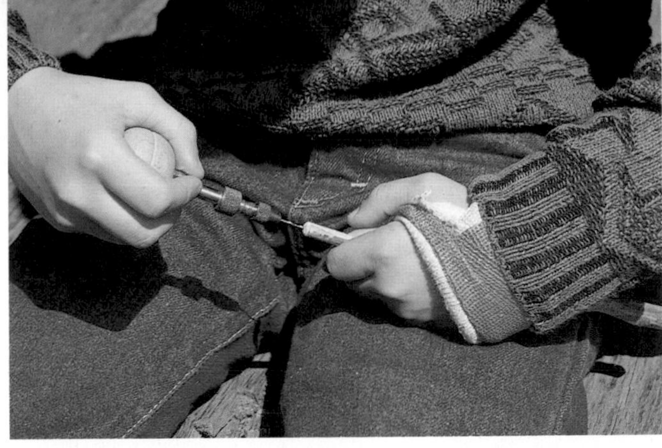

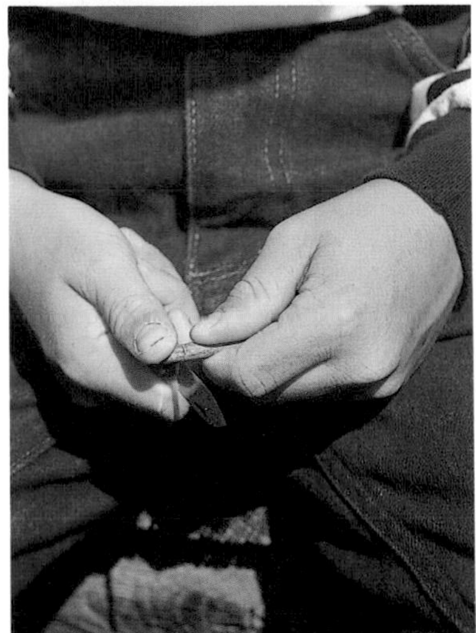

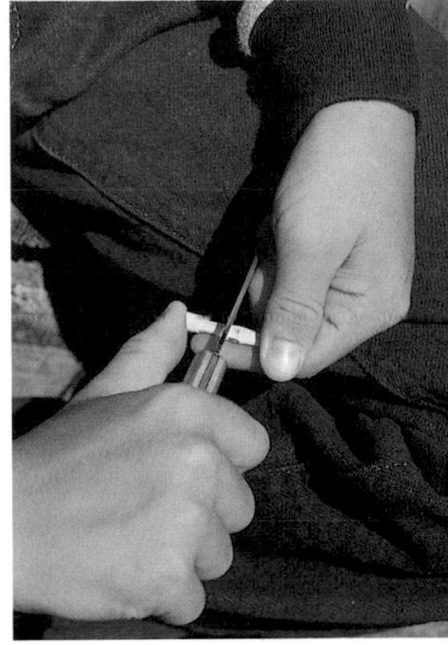

Pomander

Hundreds of years ago, people made pomanders and carried them when they visited sick people. They believed that the smell of a pomander would protect them from disease. Today we use pomanders because their delicious scent will make our closets and drawers smell good.

What You'll Need

- An orange
- Tape
- A knitting needle, a nail, or an awl
- About 1 ounce of whole cloves
- 2 feet of ribbon, cut in half

What to Do

1. Starting at the stem end, put a piece of tape around the orange. The add a second piece, so that you divide the orange into quarters. The ribbon will go over the tape path.

2. Starting next to the tape, poke holes in the orange with the knitting needle, nail, or awl, and put a clove into each hole. Put the holes as close together as possible.

3. Remove the tape and roll the pomander in powdered cinnamon, nutmeg, and ginger, to make it extra spicy. If you can find some powdered orris root—available at some natural food stores and craft stores—add it to the mixture. The orris root helps preserve the pomander.

4. Lay the ribbon in the paths you left for it, and tie up the pomander.

5. Place it in a cool, dark closet until it is hard and dry. It will shrink as it dries and will smell spicy and wonderful for years.

Scented Soap

For Clear Soap:

What You'll Need

- 2 pans, one small enough to sit inside the other
- A bar of clear, unscented glycerin soap
- 1/4 teaspoon essential oil fragrance*
- Food coloring
- Dried mint leaves, rose petals, or lavender leaves or blossoms
- Plastic cups or other small plastic containers, for molds. (The brown cups in the photo are drinking cups for camping trips.)
- Nonstick cooking spray or mineral oil

*Available at craft stores, discount marts, and health food stores.

What to Do

1. Cut the soap into small pieces, and put them in the smaller pan.
2. Get a grown-up to help you melt the soap. Fill the larger pan half full of water, bring it to a boil, and put the smaller pan with the soap inside the larger one. Stir the soap as it melts.
3. Add fragrance and color. For a very mild-smelling bar of soap, chop up some mint leaves into tiny pieces, bruise them with a mortar and pestle, and add them to the melted soap. Or crumble up dried rose petals and add them to a different bar. For a stronger scent, you'll have to use an essential oil.
4. Spray the inside of your mold with nonstick cooking spray, or grease it with mineral oil. Pour in the melted soap.
5. Place the mold in the refrigerator for a few hours. When the soap is firm, set the bottom of the mold in hot tap water for a few seconds, flex the mold, and pop out the soap.

Clear Soap

For Semisoft Soap:

What You'll Need

- A small glass custard cup or dish
- A blender
- A bar of Ivory soap or other unscented, white, floating soap
- 12 ounces of water or scented water
- 1 teaspoon essential oil (optional)
- Food coloring
- Mint leaves, lavender leaves, rose petals
- Uncooked oatmeal (if you want oatmeal scrub soap)
- Nonstick cooking spray or mineral oil

Semisoft Soap

What to Do

1. Make scented water by boiling 12 ounces of water, then pouring it over mint leaves, lavender leaves, or rose petals. Cover the water and let it steep for 15 minutes or so. (People who specialize in herbs call this water an "infusion.")

2. Cut the bar of soap into small pieces.

3. Put the soap and the water in the blender. If you want an oatmeal scrub soap, add 2 tablespoons of uncooked oatmeal.

4. Add a few drops of food coloring.

5. If you want stronger-smelling soap, add a few drops of essential oil.

6. Blend the mixture for about 15 seconds.

7. Pour the soft soap into greased dishes and let cool. When the soap is cool and somewhat solid, scoop it up in your hands and mold it into balls. It will stay semisoft, so you can pinch off pieces as you need it.

INDEX

METRIC CONVERSION CHART

Although the conversions aren't exact, there are about two and a half centimeters in an inch. So to convert inches to centimeters, just multiply the number of inches by 2.5.

To convert feet to meters, divide the number of feet by 3.25.

INCHES	MILLIMETERS
1/8	3
1/4	6
1/2	13
3/4	19

INCHES	CENTIMETERS
1	2.5
2	5
3	7.5
4	10
5	12.5
6	15
7	17.5
8	20
9	22.5
10	25
11	27.5
12	30
13	32.5
14	35
15	37.5
16	40
17	42.5
18	45
19	47.5
20	50
21	52.5
22	55
23	57.5
24	60
25	62.5
26	65
27	67.5
28	70
29	72.5
30	75